W9-CBE-520

HEAVEN'S LIGHT
BREAKING

HEAVEN'S LIGHT
BREAKING

A 25-Day Advent Devotional

GREG LAURIE

with Larry Libby

K-LOVE
BOOKS

FRANKLIN, TENNESSEE

K-LOVE BOOKS

5700 West Oaks Blvd
Rocklin, CA 95765

Published by K-LOVE Books, an imprint of EMF Publishing, LLC, 5700 West Oaks Blvd., Rocklin, CA 95765.

Published in association with the literary agency of Wolgemuth & Wilson.

Scripture quotations marked (NKJV) are taken from: *The Holy Bible*, New King James Version © 1984 by Thomas Nelson, Inc. Scripture quotations marked (NIV) are from *The Holy Bible*, New International Version®, NIV®. Copyright © 1973, 1978, 1984, 2011 by International Bible Society. Used by permission of Zondervan Publishing House. Scripture quotations marked (TLB) are taken from The Living Bible, copyright © 1971 by Tyndale House Publishers, Wheaton, Illinois. Scripture quotations marked (NLT) are taken from The New Living Translation, copyright © 1996, 2004 by Tyndale Charitable Trust. Used by permission of Tyndale House Publishers. All rights reserved. Scripture quotations marked (MSG) are taken from The Message, by Eugene Peterson. 1993, 1994, 1995, 1996, 2000, 2001, 2002. Used by permission of NavPress Publishing Group. All rights reserved. Scripture quotations marked (PHILLIPS) are from The New Testament in Modern English, Revised Edition © 1958, 1960, 1972 by J. B. Phillips. Scripture marked (TPT) are taken from The Passion Translation. Copyright © 2017, 2018, 2020 by Passion & Fire Ministries, Inc. All rights reserved. ThePassionTranslation.com.

O Come, O Come, Emmanuel: Words: various, combined by unknown author approx 12th Century, Translated by John Mason Neale, 1851. Music: 'Veni Emmanuel' 15th Century French processional. Setting: "Common Service Book" (ULCA), 1917. copyright: public domain.

Printed in the United States of America.

First edition: 2023
10 9 8 7 6 5 4 3 2 1

ISBN: 978-1-954201-48-4 (Hardcover)
ISBN: 978-1-954201-49-1 (E-book)
ISBN: 978-1-954201-50-7 (Audiobook)

Publisher's Cataloging-in-Publication Data

Names: Laurie, Greg, author.
Title: Heaven's light breaking : a 25-day advent devotional / by Greg Laurie.
Description: Includes bibliographical references. | Franklin, TN: K-Love Books, 2023.
Identifiers: ISBN: 978-1-954201-48-4 (hardcover) | 978-1-954201-49-1 (e-book) | 978-1-954201-50-7 (audio)
Subjects: LCSH Advent--Prayers and devotions. | Devotional calendars. | BISAC RELIGION / Holidays / Christmas & Advent | RELIGION / Christian Living / Devotional
Classification: LCC BV40 .L38 2023 | DDC 242/.332--dc23

Cover design by Colin Dall
Interior design by PerfecType, Nashville, TN
Author Photo by Vitaly Manzuk

CONTENTS

CONTENTS

Thousands of Years Before Bethlehem

"My King who is alive from everlasting ages past!"
Micah 5:2, TLB

Have you noticed it? Behind the scenes, many of today's scientists, historians, and educators have been working overtime trying to remove the familiar calendar designations of "BC" and "AD."

It's a small, subtle thing, of course.

But it has worlds of significance.

As we all know, BC means "Before Christ." And AD stands for *"Anno Domini,"* a Latin term meaning "Year of Our Lord." According to one keen observer, "The change was made to *mask the Christian basis for the dating system,* in a bid to accommodate non-Christians and maintain political correctness."[1] Now you are seeing BCE, which means "Before Common Era," and CE, which means "Common Era."

To put it plainly, some people want to remove Jesus—or any hint or trace of Him—from our calendars and textbooks and culture. They don't want to be reminded of His name. They don't want to admit that He was born of a virgin mother in a stable in Bethlehem. They don't want to acknowledge that He walked this earth, died on a cross, and rose from the grave. They don't want to be reminded that Jesus changed history. They don't want to admit the truth that for 2,000 years our calendars have hinged on the day of His birth.

That hinge is Christmas.

When the Son of God was born to Mary in Bethlehem of Judea, everything changed. Through time and eternity, nothing would or could ever be the same.

Christmas changed everything.

Christ changes everything—and all the politically correct scholars and "woke" writers in all the newsrooms and universities of the world can't change that truth. It is the hinge of history. When God Himself entered the world in human form, when the great Creator of the universe became a baby boy, planet Earth was transformed forever. And so were we.

Jesus, of course, did not begin life when He was conceived in Mary's womb or when He was born in that humble animal shelter. He has always existed as the Son of God, the third Person of the Trinity.

The real story of Christmas goes way, way back before Bethlehem, before Mary and Joseph, before the shepherds and wise men and innkeepers and King Herod and all of the people who played a part on that best of all nights 2,000 years ago.

How could that be? How could there be a Christmas story before Jesus came?

The answer is simply this: The story of Christmas is actually an integral part of an even greater story that goes all the way back to the beginning. It is the story of our redemption.

God had a plan to save humanity before it ever fell away from Him. God had a plan to offer salvation to you and to me before we ever saw the light of day.

Jesus knew you BC.

Think about that for a minute or two. He loved you thousands of years before Bethlehem. David the psalmist exclaimed, "You saw me before I was born and scheduled each day of my life before I began to breathe.

Every day was recorded in your book! How precious it is, Lord, to realize that you are thinking about me constantly! I can't even count how many times a day your thoughts turn toward me" (Psalm 139:16-18, TLB).

Yes, at the right moment the Lord came to us, born on a back street in the backwater town of Bethlehem. As it says in the book of Galatians: "When the fullness of the time had come, God sent forth His Son, born of a woman" (Galatians 4:4, NKJV). A better translation would be: "When the time was just right, God sent His Son. . ."

That is where He began life on earth, as the God-Man. This is where He first drew His lungs full of the air He had created. But the life of the Son of God goes back to the beginning of the beginning of the beginning. And before that! Speaking over seven centuries before the Lord's birth, the prophet Micah wrote these words:

> "But you, Bethlehem Ephrathah,
> though you are small among the clans of Judah,
> out of you will come for me
> one who will be ruler over Israel,
> whose origins are from of old,
> from ancient times."
> (Micah 5:2, NIV)

"Origins from of old!" Another translation captures it like this: "O Bethlehem Ephrathah, you are but a small Judean village, yet you will be the birthplace of my King who is alive from everlasting ages past!"[2]

The truth is, Jesus knew you and loved you before you were you.

Before your parents met.

Before your parents' parents' parents met.

Before our forefathers signed the Declaration of Independence.

Before Columbus set out from Spain.

Before Bethlehem.

Before Adam and Eve drew a breath.

Before the first star caught fire in the vault of space.

Before all Creation.

Never, never imagine that your life is random or without meaning. How could it be, when the Lord and Creator of the universe has loved you a million years before you were born.

Seven Miracle Miles

"I am First, I am Last,
I'm Alive."
Revelation 1:17-18, MSG

Did Jesus preexist before Bethlehem? Was there a Jesus before the nativity?

Yes and yes.

Bethlehem was the time and location where the incarnation took place—that is, when God began life as a human. But that is *not* when Jesus came into being. Jesus is God, and as God, He is eternal; He has always been and He always will be. In the book of Revelation, He says, "I am the First and the Last. I am the Living One; I was dead, and now look, I am alive for ever and ever!" (1:17-18, NIV).

Even though both Matthew and Luke chose to begin their Gospels with the birth of Christ, John's

Gospel begins by going back before, before, before, to the very beginning of everything.

> In the beginning was the Word, and the Word was with God, and the Word was God. He was in the beginning with God. All things were made through Him, and without Him nothing was made that was made. In Him was life, and the life was the light of men. And the light shines in the darkness, and the darkness did not comprehend it. (John 1:1-5, NKJV)

Most of our Bible translations have a definite article before the word "beginning." We read, "In the beginning was the Word . . ." In the original language, however, there is no definite article. That means you cannot pinpoint the moment in time where there was a beginning, because John is looking all the way back through time to eternity past. He is going back further than our minds can imagine.

Jesus existed before there was a world, before planets, stars, and galaxies, before light and darkness, before there was any matter whatsoever. In fact, the book of Hebrews tells us that Jesus Himself was the Author of creation. God made the world through Him.

God promised everything to the Son as an inheritance, and through the Son he created the universe. (Hebrews 1:2, NLT)

The Godhead is eternal; Jesus Christ is coequal, coeternal, and coexistent with the Father and the Holy Spirit. He was with God. He was God. He *is* God.

When Jesus entered our world as a human being, He became an embryo, and then . . . deity in diapers. Jesus left the safety of Heaven, stepped into time and space, breathed our air, shared our pain, walked in our shoes, lived our life, and died our death.

God had a face.

Jesus did not become identical to us, but He did become identified with us. In fact, He could not have identified with us any more closely than He did. It was total identification without the loss of identity, for He became one of us without ceasing to be Himself. He became human without ceasing to be God.

Jesus Christ was fully God *and* fully man. Now when I say "fully man," I don't mean He had the capacity to sin; being God, that could not or would not happen. Yet He was a man in a human body, feeling emotion, facing physical limitations, and experiencing real pain. Though actual blood coursed through His veins, He was and is deity. God in human form.

The old Christmas carol said it well:

Veiled in flesh, the Godhead see;
Hail the incarnate Deity.
Pleased as man with man to dwell
Jesus our Emmanuel. . .

John chapter 1 tells us that "the Word was with God," which literally means that "the word was *continually toward* God." This gives us a glimpse into the relationship of Father, Son, and Holy Spirit. The preposition "with" carries the idea of nearness along with a sense of movement toward God. That's another way of saying that there has always been the deepest equality and intimacy within the Trinity. Jesus summed it up in John 17:5 (NKJV), when He prayed to the Father, saying, "And now, O Father, glorify Me together with Yourself, with the glory which I had with You before the world was."

Another translation renders that verse like this:

And now, Father, glorify me
with your very own splendor,
The very splendor I had in your presence
Before there was a world. [3]

Before there was a world!

4

There was never a time when Christ did not exist. Yet this eternal Son of God became a man, and that is what we celebrate at Christmas. In Isaiah 9:6 (NKJV), written centuries before the Lord's birth, the prophet says of Him, "Unto us a Child is born; unto us a Son is given." This passage perfectly sums up what happened on Christmas, giving us both the Heavenly and the earthly perspective. We tend to view Christmas from our viewpoint: the Child being born. But then Isaiah portrays it from the Heavenly perspective: a Son is given. Christmas, then, is the story of an arrival *and* the story of a departure. He arrived on earth, but He departed from Heaven.

The theologians have a word for an appearance of God in the Old Testament: *theophany*. We might also use the word *Christophany*, which means an appearance of Christ before Bethlehem.

Are all theophanies Christophanies?

Maybe, because the apostle tells us that "No one has ever seen God. But the unique One, who is himself God, is near to the Father's heart. He has revealed God to us" (John 1:18, NLT). When God makes an appearance in the Old Testament, then, we can assume that it's Jesus, the Son of God.

How do we know He did this?

5

Consider this exchange that Jesus had with the Jewish leaders, who were all for holding onto Abraham but rejecting Jesus. The Lord speaks first here:

> "Your father Abraham rejoiced at the thought of seeing my day; he saw it and was glad."

> "You are not yet fifty years old," [the Jews] said to him, "and you have seen Abraham!"

> "Very truly I tell you," Jesus answered, "before Abraham was born, I am!" (John 8:58, NIV)

The Lord was indicating that at some point in His life, the patriarch Abraham had met Him, in what we call a pre-incarnate appearance.

For me, the account of the two disciples on the Emmaus road in the Gospel of Luke really settles the issue of Jesus making multiple appearances in the Old Testament. Do you remember that remarkable story? The two disciples were deeply dejected over what they had just seen: the arrest and crucifixion of their Lord. That's when the risen Christ Himself walked up behind them and asked why they were so despondent. And, at that moment, they didn't recognize Him. They explained to Jesus what had just happened, and how they were perplexed by reports of His missing body. It was all too sad and confusing. They decided they might as well pack up and go home to Emmaus. That's when their mysterious companion spoke up.

> Then Jesus said to them, "You foolish people! You find it so hard to believe all that the prophets wrote in the Scriptures. Wasn't it clearly predicted that the Messiah would have to suffer all these things before entering his glory?" Then Jesus took them through the writings of Moses and all the prophets, explaining from all the Scriptures the things concerning himself. (Luke 24:25-27, NLT)

Wow, wouldn't you have loved to listen in on *that* conversation? He took them through all of the passages in the Bible that allude to Messiah: The types, the pictures, and no doubt the Christophanies themselves. I wish someone could have followed about two paces behind that little group, recording them on an iPhone. (And I wish that someone could have been me.) When I get to Heaven, I would definitely love to have a conversation with Jesus just like that one.

Think of it. Those two men enjoyed the company of Jesus for seven amazing miles as they walked the dusty road from Jerusalem to the village of Emmaus. For the rest of their lives, they would never forget those seven miracle miles.

But consider this: We have something even better. We have a Savior and friend who walks with us *every mile of our lives.* He never leaves. We are never alone in life.

The One who was before time and created time will be with you through all the times of your life, until time runs into the wonders of eternity. Isn't that what the psalmist David wrote?

> "You are my God.
> My times are in your hands. . ."
> (Psalm 31:14-15, NIV)

Thanks and Praise

Lord, it's hard wrapping my mind around this: You knew me and loved me before You created the world. I can't process a concept that big. But I praise You that even if I can't wrap my thoughts around You, You have wrapped Your thoughts around me. If You were small enough for my mind, You would not be big enough for my problems. Thank You for loving me.

A Twisted Family Tree

"What are you talking about?
We're not illegitimate!"
John 8:41, TPT

The song says, "There's no place like home for the holidays . . ." Well, yes and no.

It's very true that I would rather be home with my little family at Christmas than anywhere else in the world. But "home for Christmas" can also mean getting together with extended family—relatives you don't see or have to deal with very often.

And that can be just a little bit stressful.

Let's face it, we all have weird families. We all have that obnoxious uncle, that strange aunt, those twisted cousins. And Grandpa? Well, you never know what *he's* going to say.

Maybe your parents divorced and you find yourself contending with half-brothers, half-sisters, and family members who (if you were honest) really don't seem much like family at all. Maybe you have to go visit Mom and her new boyfriend, or Dad and his new lady, and it's just a little bit awkward.

Or worse yet, they're all coming to your house and you have to get the place ready, prepare meals, and find spots for everyone to sleep. The following song was written by my friend Dennis Agajanian's father, to the tune of "Santa Claus Is Coming to Town." But he called it, "Your Relatives Are Coming to Town."

Well, you'd better give up on Christmas this year.
You haven't a chance with everyone here.
Your relatives are coming to town.

They're bringing their kids to add to your fun.
Staying ten days; you thought it was one.
Your relatives are coming to town.

They will monopolize your bathroom,
and take your solitude.
They will eat you out of house and home,
and complain about your food.
There is only one way to save your Noel,
give them your home and rent a motel.
Your relatives are coming to town.

At this time of year, people can become abnormally stressed out. I remember reading a newspaper account about a guy who had dug out his tree lights and was trying to get things sorted so they could decorate. The problem was, his wife had left the lights in a great big, tangled ball the year before, and that made him angry. He set the mess down on the driveway to go into the house for something, and while his back was turned, his teenage daughter pulled her car in and drove over the lights.

He freaked out, and started screaming at her, "Can't you see I am trying to put up the Christmas lights?" And then he told his wife he was going to go let off a little bit of steam. So he went into the backyard and started firing off rounds from his .45 caliber pistol. He was arrested for reckless endangerment and ended up in jail (which didn't improve his mood at all).

Ah . . . family troubles!

Frankly, we all have them. And people who say they don't are either delusional or outright lying. No one comes from a perfect family, because families are made up of flawed, fallible human beings.

Every now and then I hear people say, "Oh, I came from a dysfunctional home." And I have to bite my tongue to keep from saying, "Stop letting that define you! We *all* came from dysfunctional homes." Every one of us. I came from a dysfunctional home. Now I am the head of a dysfunctional home. What did you expect? That you would have parents like the Cleavers? More likely, they resemble parents like the Simpsons.

Sometimes at Christmas we're presented with ideal pictures of ideal families sitting together in ideal living rooms watching the snow fall outside, sipping cocoa, and singing carols together. And then we feel like we've fallen short because our family just doesn't look like that. Well, guess what? No one's does! You are not Jimmy Stewart or Donna Reed, and very few families today even slightly resemble the old movies. But that doesn't mean we can't build some good memories.

The fact is, every family has its share of problems, skeletons, dysfunctions, weird dynamics, and eccentric relatives.

It's popular these days to go digging into your family tree, maybe using one of those handy genealogy websites that assists you in chasing down all the roots, branches, and twigs. I have a friend who's really into this, and every time I see him, he's made some new discovery about his heritage he wants to tell me about.

There's nothing wrong with pursuing this as a hobby, as long as you remember it works both ways. You might discover that you're related to some famous general or president or royal somebody. And you also might find out that your great grandma was a madam or your grandfather's uncle was hung as a horse thief.

The human family produces as many bad apples as good ones. Probably more!

So what if you were researching your ancestors online and discovered you had a number of prostitutes populating your family tree? Is that something you'd want to tell people about? Your friend might say, "Hey, I found out that I'm a direct descendent of George Washington." Another friend might counter, "Well, I found out I come from royal blood." And you would say, "I discovered that we have three serial killers in our family tree."

Is that something you would be proud of?

Why do I bring that up? Because as we begin to delve into the most famous family tree in human history—the family tree of Jesus Christ Himself—we find liars, cheats, adulterers, and prostitutes. The

Lord's family tree had some of the most notable sinners ever, so He knows all about embarrassing relatives and dysfunctional family situations. If you think you are alone in having problems this Christmas, you can know for sure that's simply not the case.

But we also see something else at work in the family tree of our Lord.

Grace.

Powerful, incredible, restoring, wonderful grace.

The unmerited favor of God. It was at work in the family line of Jesus just as it is at work in the lives and families of everyone who calls on the Lord for salvation.

Sometimes you and I might look at our lives, sigh deeply, shake our heads, and say, "I don't think God could ever use me. I've made too many mistakes, and nothing good could come out of the mess I've made of my life. And our family? We've made so many wrong turns, and things are in a jumble. It all seems hopeless."

This family tree of Jesus in Matthew (which is actually the genealogy of Jesus' foster father, Joseph) shows, among other things, that this is simply not the case. Just look at some of the names: Rahab, the prostitute. Bathsheba, the adulteress. Ruth, the undocumented alien who wasn't even supposed to be in Israel. David, the king who committed adultery and murder. And on the list goes. The grace of God is clearly on display here.

And that same powerful grace reaches into your life and your family, right now, as you hold them up in prayer.

This is the God who brings beauty out of ashes and the Savior of the world out of a troubled and dubious family.

Thanks and Praise

Father, I am troubled for several of my family members—and You know who I am talking about. Thank You for Your grace and favor, which reaches into every distant place and every dark corner. I pray for my family—each one of them—to respond in a new and fresh way to that grace this Christmas.

DECEMBER 3

What's in a Name? (1)

"Why do you ask My name,
seeing it is wonderful?"
Judges 13:18, NKJV

What's in a name? It all depends on what your name is. If you have gone through life with a name you didn't appreciate, you know that names can really make a difference.

In the Old Testament, a man with the name of Jabez (which means "pain") made lemonade out of sour lemons. He used his name as a springboard to cry out to God for a special blessing, and the Lord answered his request.[4]

I had to go through life with the last name of Laurie—which is a girl's name, right? I would always—I mean, every time—be asked to spell it.

So maybe you, like me, went through life with a name you didn't like. Or maybe you got stuck with a nickname. Actually, names today are pretty random. Parents pick out names (or make them up) because they like how they sound—not because of what they mean.

In biblical days, names really meant something.

In the book of 1 Samuel, the wife of one of the priests gave birth to a baby in great stress when the news came that the Philistines had stolen the Ark of the Covenant. She named her baby Ichabod, meaning, "the glory has departed."

Can you imagine bringing a friend with that name home from school and introducing him to your mom? "Hey, Mom, this is my new friend, The Glory Has Departed."

But now we come to the most important name of all: the name that was given to our Lord when the angel Gabriel came to Mary and told her she would bring forth a son.

The Name Above all Names

"Do not be afraid, Mary, for you have found favor with God. And behold, you will conceive in your womb and bring forth a Son, and shall call His name JESUS. He will be great, and will be called the Son of the Highest; and the Lord God will give Him the throne of His father David. And He will reign over the house of Jacob forever, and of His kingdom there will be no end." (Luke 1:30-33, NKJV)

Jesus Christ is the name above all names—a name of great power. If you don't believe me, just say it sometime. Out loud. Say it in a crowded or even a noisy room. People might be all around you, talking like crazy. But when you say, "Jesus Christ," or "In the name of Jesus Christ," you'll be heard all over the room. People will turn to look. Conversations will stop.

The strange thing is, you could say, "Buddha," or "Hari Krishna," or even "Joseph Smith," and not create a ripple. But say the name of Jesus, and something happens in that room. Inexplicably, the dynamics change.

The Bible says that one day, at the name of Jesus Christ, every knee will bow and every tongue confess that He is the Lord, to the glory of God the Father (Philippians 2:10-11). Again, that is *every* knee, no exceptions. Napoleon will bow. So will all the kings and queens of England. Ditto with Hitler, Mao Zedong, and Osama bin Laden. Every soul in the universe will acknowledge Who He Is. For some, this will be the sweetest moment imaginable; for others, it will signal their doom.

In Isaiah 9, one of the great Christmas passages, we read a prophecy of the Lord's birth, and of the names or titles He would be given.

> *For unto us a Child is born,*
> *Unto us a Son is given;*
> *And the government will be upon His shoulder.*
> *And His name will be called*
> *Wonderful, Counselor, Mighty God,*
> *Everlasting Father, Prince of Peace.*
> *Of the increase of His government and peace*
> *There will be no end,*
> *Upon the throne of David and over His kingdom.*
> (Isaiah 9:6-7, NKJV)

Each of the names or titles for Jesus recorded in the book of Isaiah gives us an insight into who He is, but also into the purpose of God for each one of us. Think of these names like five gifts under your tree that God has for you. I am indebted to Warren Wiersbe for his excellent outline on this text *and offer the first two such gifts today, below.*

His Name Is Wonderful

This takes care of the dullness of life. The word *wonderful* comes from the root word "wonder."

Bertrand Russell once claimed that at least half of the sins of mankind were caused by a fear of boredom.

Probably the one item under most of our Christmas trees this year will be something electronic: a smart phone or tablet or smart watch or gaming system. By the time this book is printed, a new gadget will likely have hit the market—one that didn't even exist when I began writing. After all, artificial intelligence can now compose poetry, do your homework, and probably write to your mother. We have never known such advanced technology. Everywhere you go, you see people with their eyes glued to their devices, checking out Instagram, TikTok or e-mail, following Twitter, texting, or playing an addictive game. And all the while you will hear people saying, "I am really bored."

The "wonder" quickly drains away from even the latest, most cutting-edge electronic devices. In fact, they will be outdated almost from the moment they leave the shelf. Just after you buy it, you'll hear chatter about a newer version with more megapixels, apps, or battery life.

In fact, the gifts under the tree are a metaphor for life itself. After all, nothing this world has to offer will fill the voids in our lives. No matter what we own or can buy, it will never satisfy us. (Or at least, not for long.) A recent article in *USA Today* said, "Our culture is all about distraction, numbing one's self. . . There is no self-reflection, no sitting still. It is absolutely exhausting."

We need God in our lives! He is the only One who will satisfy the emptiness and the deep-down longing for "something" we can't even put words to. Scripture reminds us to "be still, and know that I *am* God" (Psalm 46:10, NKJV). *The Message* translation renders that verse: "Step out of the traffic! Take a long, loving look at me, your High God." Despite all of the passing things of this world that will not last, there is Jesus, and He is *wonderful*.

His very name is Wonder.

Life is full of letdowns, isn't it? But God is never a letdown. God is wonderful. Our awesome God takes care of the dullness of our lives. Medical science seeks to add years to our lives, but only Jesus Christ can add life to our years and give us lives worth living.

His Name Is Counselor

This takes care of the decisions of life.

Did you know that God Almighty wants to personally give you direction? That He has a plan custom-designed just for you?

Think of all the places where people look for answers today. Some go to the local bar to pour out their troubles. Some visit psychics for direction or consult a horoscope. Others will fork out money for psychiatrists, psychologists, or life coaches.

Still others will even turn to Google, typing in, *What is the meaning of life?*

Help me, Google. Isn't that sad?

I remember when I first encountered Siri, years ago, with my first iPhone. Right away, I wanted to find out what she knew. So I asked her, "What is the meaning of life?"

Siri answered, "I don't know, but I think there is an app for that." I asked her again, and she replied, "All evidence to date suggests it is chocolate."

So I said, "Siri, why am I here?" And my electronic assistant answered, "I don't know, and frankly I have been wondering that myself."

Listen. You don't need to go to Google or to Siri or to a psychic for answers about life. Everything you need to know about life and about God is found in the pages of your Bible; God will speak to you through His Word.

The Bible says of itself, "All Scripture is inspired by God and is useful to teach us what is true and to make us realize what is wrong in our lives. It corrects us when we are wrong and teaches us to do what is right. God uses it to prepare and equip his people to do every good work" (2 Timothy 3:16-17, NLT).

In Psalm 73, Asaph writes: "You guide me with your counsel, and afterward you will take me into glory" (v. 24, NIV). So, in this life and in the next, you will find no better counselor than your own Creator and Savior.

Thanks and Praise

Wonderful Counselor, speak to me in the quiet moments today. Keep me from blundering into wrong paths or foolish pursuits. How incredible to have a counselor and advocate who knows me better than I know myself, and loves me even through my missteps and failures. Guide my steps and my thoughts today!

What's in a Name? (2)

*"Everything and everyone
will one day submit to this name."*
Philippians 2:10, TPT

In the last reading, I spoke about the first of five names given to our Lord by the prophet Isaiah, some seven centuries before He was born in Bethlehem.

Looking down the centuries, Isaiah caught a glimpse of the Coming One and said, "He will be called Wonderful Counselor" (Isaiah 9:6, NIV).

But there was more. Much more. As the vision blossomed before his eyes, Isaiah added three additional names.

His Name Is Mighty God

This takes care of the demands of life.

"Power" is a big deal for men. Guys can never have too much power. If two men go to a gym, it's all about who can bench press the most or do the most curls.

Or if they're talking about a car, they're all about horsepower. I have a friend who owns a Shelby Mustang with a lot of horsepower. He let me drive it once in a big empty parking lot, and I admit, I coveted the car. With my friend riding shotgun, I put that baby in first gear, floored it, and we almost went airborne. Then I slammed it into second and threw it into third, and each time it felt like we left the ground. It was great fun!

Afterward, he told me he was having more horsepower added to it. When I asked him why in the world he would do that, he smiled and said, "Bragging rights."

It's always about power.

When you think about it, the history of mankind has been the story of acquiring, using, and abusing power. First it was manpower. Then it was horsepower, steam power, diesel power, and nuclear power. What we seem to lack is *will*power.

The Mighty God, however, is present with us to give us all the power we need to live the Christian life.

Jesus wasn't a man who became God; that would be impossible. He was and is God who became a man. The all-powerful eternal Creator and God became a baby, as difficult as it may be to wrap our minds around that thought.

That is what Christmas is all about: the astounding, incomparable moment in human history when God became a man. Jesus was and is the mighty God, which takes care of all the demands of life. All the power you will ever need to live the Christian life is available for you. As the apostle Peter wrote: "By his divine power, God has given us everything we need for living a godly life. We have received all of this by coming to know him, the one who called us to himself by means of his marvelous glory and excellence" (2 Peter 1:3, NLT).

Some people imagine that it must be hard to be a Christian. I disagree with that assessment. Actually, it is *impossible* to be a Christian. It is absolutely beyond any of us apart from the help of the Holy Spirit. With the Holy Spirit, however, God will help you be the man or woman He has called you to be. As the Bible says, "With God all things are possible."[5]

Many people will open electronic gizmos this Christmas only to find that their new toys don't work. So they will look up the phone number or website for tech support and chat with someone. Those technicians are usually trained to ask two questions first: "Is the device plugged in? Is the device turned on?" You would be amazed by how many people's devices "don't work" because they're not plugged in or turned on.

God might ask the same of us. Are you plugged in? God will give you the power to live the life He has called you to live.

His Name Is Everlasting Father

That takes care of the future of life.

We know that life is more than what we are currently experiencing. In fact, the Bible teaches that you and I will live forever. That's a good thing, right?

Not necessarily.

It all depends on *where* you will live forever. You are an eternal soul. You are not a body that happens to have a soul; you are, as C. S. Lewis put it, a soul wrapped in a body. And the Bible teaches that one day your life on earth will end, and if you're a believer in Jesus Christ, your soul and your resurrected body will go into God's presence in Heaven, where you will live with Him forever. But if you are not a believer, the Bible teaches that you will spend all eternity separated from God in a place called hell.

If you know the Everlasting Father, however, you don't have to be afraid of that.

Do you know Him in this way? Maybe you never got a chance to know your earthly father, which perhaps makes Christmas a difficult season. Maybe your dad walked out on the family and you haven't seen him in years. Perhaps you were estranged from him at some point, and you have a strained relationship with him right now. You think of God being Father, and it's difficult for you to relate.

I can understand that.

I never had a father growing up and never knew my real dad. I was conceived out of wedlock, and then my mom married and divorced seven different guys—and only one of them ever treated me as a father would. He was the one who adopted me and gave me my name, Laurie. So I had a love for that man and was able to go back later in life, locate him, and lead him to Christ.

When I came to Jesus Christ, it was so great to realize that there was a Father in Heaven who would always be there for me, never abandon me, never desert me, and always take time for me.

When my father who adopted me died, God was there. When my mother died, God was there. When the most devastating event of my life happened—the death of my son Christopher in an automobile accident—I wondered if I could survive it. But again, God was there. He has always been there for me and always will be.

And He will always be there for you because He is your Everlasting Father.

His Name Is Prince of Peace

This takes care of the disturbances of life.

In the storms of life, we long for peace. Life is filled with friction, hardship, and difficulty. We see troubled homes, troubled cities, and troubled people everywhere. But Jesus will be the Prince of Peace in your life. You won't find peace in a bottle, in a drug, in a political persuasion, in a human relationship, or in material possessions. You will only find peace in a relationship with God through Jesus Christ.

We remember the message that the angels gave to the shepherds, keeping watch over their flocks by night: "Glory to God in the highest, and on earth peace, goodwill toward men!" (Luke 2:14, KJV).

Yet when we look around our world at all the turmoil, strife, and anguish, we might find ourselves asking, "Where is it? Where is that peace?" Even the town of Bethlehem is now often unsafe at night. Where is the peace the angels promised? Was it a joke? Were they mocking us?

No.

That statement of the angels could better be translated, "Glory to God in the highest, and peace on earth *among men with whom God is well-pleased.*"

You see, all of the problems we witness and experience in the world today are the result of man and his disobedience to God. Humanity itself has brought about the violence, unrest, turmoil, and war on the planet. But despite those things, you and I can have peace in the midst of the most troubled times and difficult situations.

Even when chaos rages all around, even in the middle of the storm, you can have peace because the Lord *is* your peace. In John 14, Jesus said, "I am leaving you with a gift—peace of mind and heart. And the peace I give is a gift the world cannot give. So don't be troubled or afraid" (v. 27, NLT).

Do you have this peace that Jesus spoke of? The Bible describes it as the peace that passes all human understanding. But before you can have the peace *of* God you must first have peace *with* God, through Jesus Christ.

So what is in a name? It all depends on whose name it is. If it is the name of Jesus Christ, everything you need is in that name. The Bible says, "whoever calls on the name of the LORD shall be saved" (Acts 2:21, NKJV).

His name is Wonderful.

Thanks and Praise

Lord, even if I lost everything tonight, I would still have You as my companion. I would still have a heart and conscience made clean by Your sacrifice for me. I would still have the hope of Heaven and eternal life. I praise You for adopting me as Your own and walking with me through all my days.

Gabriel's First Call

"Don't be afraid, Zechariah!
God has heard your prayer."
Luke 1:13, NLT

It was a day like any other when the supernatural invaded the natural.

Zechariah, the priest, stood in the temple in Jerusalem, performing his priestly duties. The Gospel of Luke tells us that "his order was on duty that week. As was the custom of the priests, he was chosen by lot to enter the sanctuary of the Lord and burn incense. While the incense was being burned, a great crowd stood outside, praying" (Luke 1:8-10, NLT).

So here was this gray-bearded senior citizen, bringing the offering on behalf of the people of Israel. Many priests served in the nation at that time, so he would have considered it a high honor and real privilege. He probably looked forward to going home that night and telling his wife, Elizabeth, all about it—what it had felt like to be in that holy place, representing the people before the God of Israel.

As it turned out, he had more to tell Elizabeth than he would have ever dreamed. The only trouble was, after that day, he wouldn't be able to speak!

As Zechariah ministered in the temple, a mighty angel of the Lord, fresh from the brilliant glory of Heaven, suddenly appeared to him, standing at the right side of the altar of incense. Understandably, Zechariah was startled and probably froze in position with fear.

That's when the angel began to speak:

"Don't be afraid, Zechariah! God has heard your prayer. Your wife, Elizabeth, will give you a son, and you are to name him John. You will have great joy and gladness, and many will rejoice at his birth, for he will be great in the eyes of the Lord. He must never touch wine or other alcoholic drinks. He will be filled with the Holy Spirit, even before his birth. And he will turn many Israelites to the Lord their God. He will be a man with the spirit and power of Elijah. He will prepare the people for the coming of the Lord. He will turn the hearts of the fathers to their children, and he will cause those who are rebellious to accept the wisdom of the godly." (Luke 1:13-17, NLT)

The angel says, "God has heard your prayer . . ." The way this verse reads in the original language seems to imply that God heard the prayer that Zechariah had been praying *at that very moment.*

Was he praying about having a son? Had he been expressing the secret longing of his heart to the Lord? Had he prayed that God might take away Elizabeth's disgrace among other women and allow her to bear a child? It's possible, but then, why was he so doubtful when it was revealed to him that he and Elizabeth were going to have a boy?

Then again, Zechariah may have been praying for the Messiah to arrive and finally deliver Israel. Many of his godly countrymen longed for the Promised One to come and deliver them from the iron heel of Rome. Perhaps Zechariah was praying in his heart, saying, "Lord, hear the prayers of Your people, gathered outside this temple. They long for a Messiah. They long for a deliverer and a Savior. Won't You please send Him to us?"

Suddenly Gabriel appeared, with news about that Messiah—and with an exciting personal word for Zechariah and his wife. Again, Gabriel had said, "God has heard your prayer . . ."

To those of us who have walked with the Lord

for years, it's not a surprise to hear that God answers prayer; we've seen countless answers to the specific requests and concerns we bring before the Lord. But sometimes it does surprise us when God answers our prayers *right away.*

Have you ever prayed for something and found yourself shocked when God answered it almost immediately?

We've all experienced times when God doesn't say yes or no to our request, but something more like, "Wait." He is saying, in effect, "That is a good request, but you aren't ready for that right now." At other times God will hear our prayer and say, "No, My child, I love you too much to give you what you just asked for."

Then there are times when the prayer is hardly out of our mouth and the answer comes. Bam! It's there! The phone rings, or there's a knock on the door, or a letter arrives, or an e-mail pops up, and we receive the very thing we were just praying about.

If the truth were known, you and I often pray with a measure of doubt in our hearts. There is a good illustration of this in Acts 12, where James and Peter had both been arrested by King Herod and James had been put to death. When fellow believers heard that James was gone, I'm sure they prayed with all their hearts for Peter, that God would somehow deliver him from almost certain death.

Did they realize God was actually listening?

In a direct answer to their prayers, He dispatched an angel, who went to Peter's prison cell in the night. A Heavenly light shone in that dark dungeon, and the iron shackles fell off Peter's wrists and his legs. The door opened of its own accord, just like it does at Walmart, and Peter walked out of prison right past the sleeping guards and sentries.

Once out of jail, Peter hurried over to the house of John Mark, where he knew people would be praying. Looking this way and that to make sure he wasn't being followed, Peter knocked on the door, and a servant girl named Rhoda answered.

She opened the door, and there stood the very answer to their prayers!

Instead of inviting him in, however, she closed the door in his face and excitedly ran into the back room, where men and women were praying for Peter with all their might.

"Oh, Lord, be merciful to Peter."

"Lord, please deliver our brother Peter."

"God, Peter needs You right now. We pray for a miracle."

And at that very moment, the miracle they were praying for was still knocking on the door, trying to get in. When Rhoda gave the news, they told her she was crazy. How could Peter be at the door when he was in prison? Silly girl. It wasn't possible. Rhoda was seeing things.

But Rhoda kept insisting, "Guys, I'm telling you right now that *Peter* is standing at the front door!" Scripture tells us (and I love this) that they *all* went to the front door. The whole group.

The Bible says that when they saw Peter, "they were astonished."

If I were Peter, I think I'd be just a little bit sarcastic, saying, "Hello, everybody, were you going to leave me out here all night?"

These were good people who prayed fervently, but they must have prayed with some doubt too. When God answered their prayer so quickly, they were amazed.

I don't know what you may be facing right now, as another Christmas rolls around. I don't know what burdens you might be carrying on your shoulders or what sort of complications or trials you might be enduring. You need to bring those things continually before the Lord in prayer. The

Bible tells us, "Don't worry about anything; instead, pray about everything. Tell God what you need, and thank him for all he has done. Then you will experience God's peace, which exceeds anything we can understand. His peace will guard your hearts and minds as you live in Christ Jesus" (Philippians 4:6-7, NLT).

Let's look back at Zechariah. Remember that as Zechariah prayed, God heard him, dispatching the angel Gabriel with the answer.

It's just a little bit amazing to me that Zechariah would have an angelic visitation, awesome as that must have been, and *still* express doubt about God answering his prayer.

Zechariah said to the angel, "How can I be sure this will happen? I'm an old man now, and my wife is also well along in years."

Then the angel said, "I am Gabriel! I stand in the very presence of God. It was he who sent me to bring you this good news! But now, since you didn't believe what I said, you will be silent and unable to speak until the child is born. For my words will certainly be fulfilled at the proper time." (Luke 1:18-19, NLT)

Zechariah is saying, "Well, hmmm, let's see. Have you considered the fact that I'm pretty old for something like that to happen? Does God realize that my wife is no spring chicken either?"

I could find myself becoming pretty critical of Zechariah—until I remember all the mighty things God has shown me through the years of my life, all the incredible answers to prayer I have seen, and yet I still struggle with doubt sometimes.

In the meantime, people outside the temple sanctuary were getting a little restless, wondering why the old fellow was taking so long. Had he died in there? Had a stroke? What in the world was going on?

Suddenly, Zechariah emerged. And he couldn't speak! The Bible says, "Then they realized from his gestures and his silence that he must have seen a vision in the sanctuary" (Luke 1:22, NLT). Did you ever wonder what kind of gestures Zechariah made to explain what he had seen? Did he flap his arms up and down to indicate "angel"?

Whatever happened outside the sanctuary, Zechariah knew very well what had happened inside. First of all, wonder of wonders, he was going to be a daddy after all. (They would have to make his den into a nursery!) Even more significant, his little boy would grow up to be the forerunner of the Messiah. Which meant the long-awaited Deliverer of Israel couldn't be far behind.

It was game on. The story was beginning to unfold. Messiah was on His way.

Thanks and Praise

Father, thank You for all the many answers to prayers I have seen. Thank You for the times You answered before I even finished praying. If I could really grasp how powerful You are and how ready You are to respond, maybe I would spend more time seeking You and asking.

Gabriel's Second Call

"Good morning!
You're beautiful with God's beauty,
Beautiful inside and out!
God be with you."
Luke 1:28, MSG

Mary was the most privileged woman who ever lived. Can anyone doubt that?

Yet she did not live a privileged life. In fact, she lived in what you might call a "nothing town" in the middle of nowhere.

Here is how her story began:

Now in the sixth month the angel Gabriel was sent by God to a city of Galilee named Nazareth, to a virgin betrothed to a man whose name was Joseph, of the house of David. The virgin's name was Mary. And having come in, the angel said to her, "Rejoice, highly favored one, the Lord is with you; blessed are you among women!" (Luke 2:26-28, NKJV)

There has been a great deal of misunderstanding about Mary through the centuries. On one hand, she has been placed high on a pedestal. Some would even say we should pray to her and through her to Jesus, which of course Scripture does not teach. But then on the other hand, some people simply ignore her or misunderstand her place in this greatest of stories.

We need to strip away some of the traditional trappings of Christmas to see Mary's true place for what it is. What can we learn from this young woman's life?

Mary was a Godly Young Woman Living in a Godless Place

Did you know that it's possible to live a godly life, even though you live, work, or go to school in an ungodly environment? Mary proved that. Where did she live? Nazareth.

Nazareth, along with Bethlehem, has been romanticized by believers down through the years. But what was it really like when Mary and Joseph lived there?

It wasn't what you call a destination resort.

Far from it.

If Hollywood had been telling it, or if the Christmas story had been stage-managed by a public relations firm, Jesus would have been born in Rome. Why? Because Rome was the powerful, sophisticated capital of a great world empire. The child Jesus would have grown up in a marble villa wearing a pure white toga, edged in gold.

But God didn't choose a girl from Rome. Nor did God choose a girl from Athens, the intellectual and cultural capital of the world. He didn't even choose a girl from Jerusalem, home of the great temple and spiritual capital of Israel.

He picked a teenage girl from Nazareth.

Nazareth at that time was overrun by Roman soldiers. It was a place known for wickedness and sin, where people built pagan temples for the worship of countless false gods. Someday an archaeologist digging through the rubble of ancient Nazareth will probably come across the slogan, "What happens in Nazareth stays in Nazareth."

In fact, Nazareth was one of those places you pass through when you're on your way to somewhere else. I'm reminded a little of Barstow,

California. If you happen to be from Barstow, I mean no offense. It's a nice little spot and even has an In-N-Out Burger—a great place to pull off the road and get some gas or check your GPS. Most people, however, pass *through* Barstow on the way to somewhere else. Most people don't go there as a destination. It's out in the middle of the desert! That's what Nazareth was like: an obscure, off-the-beaten-path kind of place.

Unlike Barstow, however, Nazareth was known for its sin and wickedness. That explains Nathanael's reaction when he heard that Jesus was from Nazareth. He said, "Can anything good come out of Nazareth?" (John 1:46, NKJV)

So as Jesus grew up, He became known as "Jesus of Nazareth."

"Jesus of Jerusalem" would have rolled off the tongue a little nicer. People might have sat up and took notice, thinking, *Well, maybe He has something to say, because He is from a great spiritual center.* Or maybe "Jesus of Rome." People might have thought, *He probably knows some important people. He's probably well-connected.*

But "Jesus of Nazareth"?

Well, that wasn't impressive. And it was just a little bit embarrassing.

Nevertheless, God picked Mary and this obscure place to accomplish His purpose. He picked an unknown girl living in an unknown place to bring about the most known event in human history: The birth of the Lord Jesus Christ.

What do we learn from this? We learn that God seems to go out of His way to pick the most unexpected person to accomplish His goals. He seems to go out of His way to choose the most ordinary individual to do the most extraordinary things.

I like the way Paul said it in 1 Corinthians 1:26-28: "Take a good look, friends, at who you were when you got called into this life. I don't see many of 'the brightest and the best' among you, not many influential, not many from high-society families. Isn't it obvious that God deliberately chose men and women that the culture overlooks and exploits and abuses, chose these 'nobodies' to expose the hollow pretensions of the 'somebodies'?" (MSG).

We forget that sometimes—even when we're thinking about the "greats" of the Bible, like David, Gideon, Deborah, or the apostle Peter. We forget that they became prominent *because of what God did through them*, not because they were great in themselves. When God called him, David was a shepherd boy watching over his dad's flock. He was so lightly regarded in his own family that his father had to be strongly prompted even to acknowledge him. Yet God said, "David will be the next king of Israel."

When God chose Gideon, calling him a "mighty man of valor," he was hiding from his enemies in a wine press. God called Deborah to make a difference in her time. Scripture says, "Villagers in Israel would not fight; they held back until I, Deborah, arose, until I arose, a mother in Israel" (Judges 5:7, NIV). When God called Simon Peter, he was just a regular blue-collar working stiff, out in a boat trying to keep his fishing business going. Yet the Lord raised him up to be one of the great apostles.

Why does God do this? First Corinthians 1:28-29 provides the answer: "God chose things despised by the world, things counted as nothing at all, and used them to bring to nothing what the world considers important. As a result, no one can ever boast in the presence of God" (NLT).

Here's the point: God can use ordinary people. In fact, God *prefers* and delights to use people like you and me to get the job done and advance His kingdom. So don't ever think of yourself as a nobody out in the middle of nowhere. God knows exactly who you are, where you are, and why you are. He cares deeply about you, and He can use you in ways beyond what you might have imagined.

Mary is a prime example. He chose an unknown girl from a poorly regarded place to give birth to the King of kings.

Thanks and Praise

Praise You, Lord, that You aren't impressed by a person's wealth, fame, education, or pedigree—or even gifts and talents. Thank You that You can use ordinary people who simply love You and want to serve You. Please use me, today, Lord, in whatever way You choose.

Questions and Answers

"I am the Lord's servant. . . .
May your word to me be fulfilled."
Luke 1:38, NIV

Most of us will never see an angel until we step across the threshold of Heaven. And then, it seems, we'll find angels almost everywhere we look. On that glorious day when we open our eyes to our final home, we will see "thousands upon thousands of angels in joyful assembly." Or as another translation puts it, Heaven will be "populated by throngs of festive angels and Christian citizens" (Hebrews 12:22, NIV, MSG)

So it was an experience of a lifetime for Mary to see an angel. But the words the angel spoke to her were even more stunning. Gabriel greeted her as "highly favored one." In Luke 1:29 (NKJV), we read that "when she saw him, she was troubled at his saying, and considered what manner of greeting this was."

In other words, she was thoroughly shaken, and she couldn't imagine what such a greeting would mean for her.

The wording of this verse in some translations has led to many misunderstandings. In these versions, Gabriel says, "Hail Mary, full of grace, the Lord is with you, blessed are you among women." That has even become a prayer to some. But the truth is, Gabriel is not saying, "Hail Mary" as in "Praise Mary." A better translation would simply be, "Greetings, Mary." What's more, the angel wasn't saying that grace was emanating from Mary, but rather that God had extended His grace to her. And what is grace? It is the unmerited favor of God.

Yes, Mary was most blessed among women. But Mary was also a normal human being and a sinner like everyone else. She was not born of immaculate conception; that is nowhere even hinted at in Scripture. Mary herself, in her joyous psalm of praise that she offered after she realized she would be the mother of the Messiah, said, "My soul rejoices in *God my Savior.*"

In other words, Mary needed a Savior like everyone else.

But why would a powerful heavenly emissary greet her in that way, calling her "highly favored"? She was just a teenage girl in a no-account town. She must have said to herself, *It's so overwhelming! I am to be the one. I will be the fulfillment of Bible prophesy.* Perhaps she quoted Isaiah 7:14 (NKJV) in her mind, "Behold, the virgin shall conceive and bear a Son, and shall call His name Immanuel."

And she was going to be *that* virgin. And by the way, the word here used for virgin really does mean *virgin.* If you have a translation that says "handmaiden" or "young woman," that is not correct. She had never been involved sexually with a man.

But then Mary had a question for the angel—and a very logical question under the circumstances: "But how can this happen? I am a virgin" (Luke 1:34, NLT).

In other words, "With all due respect, Mr. Gabriel, sir, how could this happen? I have never had sex with a man." Mary was humble and reflective, and after she'd thought about it, she asked the logical question.

Mary wasn't doubting as Zechariah did when he was told he would be the father of John. This question had more to do with biology. She wasn't questioning Gabriel; she was only questioning the methodology. *How does this work?* And because it was an honest, legitimate question, Gabriel answered her.

"The Holy Spirit will come upon you, and the power of the Most High will overshadow you. So the baby to be born will be holy, and he will be called the Son of God" (Luke 1:35, NLT).

Sometimes we ask "How?" questions of God too. How can I live a godly life in this kind of culture? How can I as a single person remain sexually pure and wait for God to bring that right person to me? How can I as a married person remain faithful to my spouse, attentive to my kids, honest in my work, and uncompromised in my principles? How can I survive this crisis I'm experiencing right now?

How does it work, Lord? How do I put life together?

Gabriel has the answer for Mary, and for us, in verse 37: "For with God nothing will be impossible" (NKJV).

Remember that truth! He will complete the work He has begun in your life.

The angel said, "The Holy Spirit will come upon you, Mary." And the Holy Spirit comes upon us as well, doesn't He? In fact, the Bible tells us that we are to be filled with the Holy Spirit. Filled and refilled and refilled. Every day. Every hour. Every moment.

God will give us the power to do what He has called us to do (2 Peter 1:3).

After absorbing this absolutely incredible news, Mary finally replied: "I am the Lord's servant. May everything you have said about me come true" (Luke 1:38, NLT).

In other words, "It's a done deal, Lord. You just tell me where and when." Did she fully understand all the implications? Of course not! But what she did understand, she submitted to.

I love it that she didn't demand a detailed explanation of how it would all play out. She didn't say, "Wait. Wait. Wait. How will this work? How are we going to get Joseph on board with this? How is this going to appear to others? And what about this? And what about that?" No, she simply submitted to the word of the Lord.

In our lives, there are many times when we want to know God's will before we will submit to it. We want a detailed explanation—to read the fine print before we sign on the dotted line. We want to know if there is an escape clause!

The fact is, if you want to know God's will for your life, you need to first surrender yourself to Him. Without detailed information. Without a roadmap.

Alan Redpath has wisely said, "The condition of an enlightened mind is a surrendered heart." It is the man or woman with a surrendered heart who will know the will of God.

Mary did that. She submitted her will to God, despite not knowing the details and complications.

And there certainly were complications.

Again, sometimes we romanticize this story and don't think of Mary and Joseph as real flesh and blood people. Mary was hardly more than a girl; some commentators believe she was as young as twelve, or perhaps as old as fourteen. She was a young teen called by God, and now she had the task of giving this account to Joseph, her husband-to-be.

Back in those days you didn't choose your own mate; your parents chose for you. Most likely, Mary and Joseph were still small children when their parents made the decision that they would be a good match. And so she was espoused to Joseph, which meant that one day they would be married. From childhood, then, he knew who his wife was going to be, and she knew who her husband was going to be.

And now she is pregnant and must explain this to Joseph.

We're not given her words in Scripture, but I imagine them going something like this: "Joseph, I know this is going to sound strange, but an angel has come to me and told me that I am to be with child by the Holy Spirit, and that the Spirit Himself will bring this about. If you can believe it, *I am* the virgin with child from Isaiah 7:14. And you need to know that absolutely nothing else has gone on. I promise you that! Joseph . . . are you OK with this?"

He wasn't OK with it.

Who would be?

Joseph was heartbroken and made up his mind to divorce Mary quietly and somehow move on in life. But then he also received an angelic visitation, in a dream, at night. Was it Gabriel? The Bible doesn't say. But the message was clear:

> *"Joseph, son of David," the angel said, "do not be afraid to take Mary as your wife. For the child within her was conceived by the Holy Spirit. And she will have a son, and you are to name him Jesus, for he will save his people from their sins." (Matthew 1:20-21, NLT)*

Because Joseph wanted to do the right and honorable thing, the Lord kept him from doing what would have been the wrong thing: divorcing Mary. Instead, the angel not only reassured Joseph's heart about Mary's faithfulness, but he also gave Joseph a glimpse of the Baby's future and what He would accomplish for His people.

God had a vast, wonderful, and intricate plan concerning the birth of His Son. It took His power and His wisdom to pull it off. As Isaiah 9:7 (NKJV) predicted: "The zeal of the LORD of hosts will perform this."

That was the divine element.

But the very human element began with a godly young girl who looked into the face of impossibility and said, "Whatever you want, Lord. That's what I will do."

Thanks and Praise

Thank You, Lord, for this example. Thank You for the way Mary accepted Your plan, even though she had no idea how it could happen or how it would work out. Help me today to walk in Your will and plan for my life, trusting You with all the details that don't make sense yet.

Home for Christmas

*"There is plenty of room for you in my Father's home.
If that weren't so, would I have told you
that I'm on my way to get a room ready for you?"*
John 14:2, MSG

I'll be home for Christmas, you can count on me . . ."
I don't know what comes to your mind when you hear the word *home*, but for many years of my life, I didn't really have a place I could call "home." We lived in dumpy little houses, we lived in apartments, and sometimes we lived with other people. Mine was a broken home. My mother was married and divorced seven times, and she was always going from husband to husband.

We moved from California to New Jersey, to Hawaii, and then back to California again. Mom was out drinking every night, so I never knew what it was like to have a family meal. I got my own food at a burger joint near our apartment, always ordering the exact same thing: a hamburger, vanilla malt, and French fries.

One Christmas morning stays with me. We had one of those white, artificial trees with the little light that slowly turns and changes colors, with some funky song endlessly repeating. My mother was passed out from a night of drinking, and the house smelled of stale smoke and alcohol. As I sat there looking at that pitiful tree and at my mom, I thought to myself, *It's got to get better than this.*

And it did. Did it ever! In the Lord's grace and kindness, I met Cathe Martin, later to become Laurie, and we got married. That was the first time I knew what a home was. We didn't have a fancy place at all in those days, just a little shoebox house with threadbare furniture from The Salvation Army. We had two sons, and when I was with Cathe and my boys we were *home*. That was the real thing for me. And it still is.

Through my years as a pastor, I've been in huge, palatial houses that really weren't homes at all, and I've been in humble structures that you would barely even call a house—but one with all the warmth and comfort of a real home.

When Jesus, the Son of God, walked this earth you could technically say He was homeless. He said, "Foxes have dens to live in, and birds have nests, but the Son of Man has no place even to lay his head" (Matthew 8:20, NLT).

Before Bethlehem, however, He had the greatest of homes we could ever imagine. I love the way the apostle Paul described it: "You know how full of love and kindness our Lord Jesus was: though he was so very rich, yet to help you he became so very poor, so that by being poor he could make you rich" (2 Corinthians 8:9, TLB).

In John 14 Jesus said, "My Father's house has many rooms; if that were not so, would I have told you that I am going there to prepare a place for you? And if I go and prepare a place for you, I will come back and take you to be with me that you also may be where I am" (vv. 2-3, NIV).

"My Father's house" suggests something big, like a vast, spacious estate. But the word "rooms" suggests coziness, a private space. (Think of it: He has prepared a room for each of us. He's been working on it for 2,000 years!)

Here's my point: Jesus left His home in Heaven so *you* could have a home in Heaven. God sent His

Son from the infinite beauty of Heaven to be born in the most crude, unsanitary conditions imaginable. God went from the glory of the throne to a feeding trough in a cold, damp cave with the animals and the smell of urine in the air.

It was an unwelcoming place, but in my mind that doesn't diminish the Christmas story at all. In fact, it enhances the story to think of all that God left to come to us. What an amazing sacrifice.

He left His Heavenly home so we could have a Heavenly home. He left His home in Heaven to make a home in our hearts. He was born so we could be born again. As C. S. Lewis put it in *Mere Christianity*: "The Son of God became a man to enable men *to* become sons of God."[6]

When a man or woman becomes a Christian, Jesus Christ takes residence in his or her heart. Don't let anyone tell you something different; that is exactly what the Bible teaches.

I heard the story of a mother who told her little girl, "Jesus lives in my heart." So the little girl put her ear to her mom's chest and said, "I am listening to Jesus in your heart." And the mother said, "Really? What are you hearing?" She says, "Mom, I think right now He's making coffee." Maybe the mother had indigestion. I don't know. But the fact is, when a person believes in Jesus, He lives inside of you through the presence of the Holy Spirit.

Colossians 1:27 (NLT) says, "And this is the secret: Christ lives in you. This gives you assurance of sharing his glory." And then in John 1:12 (NIV) we read: "Yet to all who did receive him, to those who believed in his name, he gave the right to become children of God." In John 14:23 (NLT), "All who love me will do what I say. My Father will love them, and we will come and make our home with each of them."

Is Jesus at home—*really at home*—in your heart?

Let me explain what I mean by that. Writing to the church in Ephesus, Paul said, "I pray . . . that Christ may dwell in your hearts through faith. And I pray that you, being rooted and established in love, may have power, together with all the Lord's holy people, to grasp how wide and long and high and deep is the love of Christ."[7]

Now here's a question: Why would Paul pray that Christ would dwell in the hearts of people who had already put their faith in Christ? Doesn't He already dwell in the heart of every man and woman who has received him? The answer is yes, but we need to understand what the word *dwell* means. It's a compound word—so, basically a prayer that Christ may "settle down and be at home in your life."

Is that true for you this Christmas? Has He settled down and made Himself "at home" in your life?

It's a valid question. Have you ever walked into someone's home and found yourself ill at ease? As soon as you stepped across the threshold, something put you off. Maybe what was playing on TV. Maybe the music on the sound system. Maybe the smell of cooked cabbage or liver and onions. Whatever it was, you felt uncomfortable and wanted to leave.

But then again, have you ever been in a home that felt welcoming from the time you walked through the door? The atmosphere felt warm and relaxed, you smelled something great cooking on the stove, and everyone seemed glad to see you. They said, "Please, take off your coat. Sit down. Spend a little time with us."

Is Jesus settled down and at home in your heart— or is there something in your life that would cause Him to be ill at ease? Are there things you would want to put away so He wouldn't see them? Would you still feel comfortable continuing to watch that show on Netflix if Jesus suddenly walked into the room?

Sometimes you hear the Spanish expression, *mi casa es su casa*, which means "my house is your house." When you become a Christian, that literally becomes true. Jesus doesn't want to be a guest in your home; He claims ownership. When you invite Him into your life, He is the one who owns the house. You are living in *His* house. As Tennyson wrote in "The Higher Pantheism": "Closer is He than breathing, and nearer than hands and feet."[8]

And wherever He lives, He brings peace and joy along with Him.

Thanks and Praise

Praise You, Lord, that I don't have to look for You in faraway places or travel to some shrine or holy place to find You. You are with me, as near as my next heartbeat, my next breath. Open my mind, Lord, to the reality of Your presence with me and in me.

People Who Missed Christmas

"How often I have longed to gather
your children together . . .
[but] you were not willing."
Luke 13:34, NIV

What the tired couple needed when they came into Bethlehem was a nice motel. Or just any motel. A Motel 6 would have been fine, but they would have settled for a Motel 72! As they made their weary way through town, however, all they could see on every hand were "No Vacancy" signs. They came to the inn where they had hoped to stay, but there was no room for them, and they were turned away.

Presumably, an innkeeper delivered this bad news. Clearly, he could see that Mary was well along in her pregnancy and that she needed a clean and warm room in case she was to give birth.

But he stood at the door of the inn and shook his head. "Sorry," he said, "not tonight. No room. Nothing available."

And then he closed the door.

It was the worst decision of his whole life.

The Innkeeper Missed Christmas

Frankly, it's hard for me to imagine a man being that heartless, turning away an obviously pregnant young woman and her husband. It seems like just simple human kindness would say, *Clear a space for these two. Put a roof over them. Put up a tent. Do something! She could give birth tonight.*

If he had only known. In this woman's womb was the creator of a billion galaxies in human form. And this hassled hospitality worker was too busy to give them the time of day, much less a place of rest and shelter.

If you were Joseph, with responsibility for this woman and the unborn child, you would have found yourself saying, *Now what?* As it turned out, there was a ramshackle little building—or perhaps a cave—behind the inn that was used to stable animals. With no other options, Joseph finally sought shelter there for the night.

As Admiral Horatio Nelson would say some 2,000 years later, "Desperate affairs require desperate measures." Joseph had to do something. It wasn't an option to have the baby in the street.

It's easy to vilify the innkeeper. More plausibly, he was simply preoccupied and busy. Occupied with making money, he had all the business he could handle that night.

It reminds me of our country today and those who have no time to seek God. You invite people to church and they reply, "We're just too busy right now. We have so much to do."

We say, "Why don't you come to church with us on Christmas?"

And we hear replies like, "That's a nice idea but we're going to a play or this movie just opened we have to do a bit more shopping or we have another commitment."

I'm reminded of the psalmist, who wrote about a man who couldn't be bothered with seeking the Lord: "In all his thoughts there is no room for God" (Psalm 10:4, NIV).

So it is with many in today's world. Even on the day set aside to celebrate the birth of Jesus Christ, there's no time for Him. Nothing left in the schedule. No time for faith. No room in the inn.

So, the Savior of the world was born in a barn.

But it wasn't Jesus who missed out, it was the innkeeper. Why did he miss out? Because he was likely interested in the bottom line. The dollar. The buck. Or in his case the shekel. So in the busyness of all that was going on with the census being taken, he missed the coming of the Messiah and Savior of the world. And he missed Christ. Just like so many people today.

Just for a moment, can you imagine if it had gone differently and the innkeeper had made a deep personal sacrifice to help Mary and Joseph? What if compassion had welled up in his heart, and he had given up his own room, his own bed, and offered this needy couple a free evening meal?

I don't know for sure, but I imagine that his story would have been included in Scripture, and that men and women and boys and girls would have repeated it all over the world, down through the centuries. In all the Christmas plays for all time, everyone would want to be the innkeeper.

That's what happened to the lady who sacrificed her precious alabaster jar of perfume and poured it on the soon-to-be-crucified Messiah. In response, the Lord told His disciples, "She will always be remembered for this deed. The story of what she has done will be told throughout the whole world, wherever the Good News is preached" (Matthew 26:13, TLB). And so it has been, for over 2,000 years.

In the book of Jonah, the prophet made this statement: "Those who cling to worthless idols forfeit the grace that could be theirs."[9] The innkeeper held onto his money and his comfort that first Christmas night. But he forfeited a privilege that would have lasted forever.

The Religious Leaders Missed Christmas

When the magi arrived in Jerusalem, seeking the child who was born King of the Jews, Herod called on his brain trust of theological experts and asked where the Messiah would be born.

They knew the answer right away: Bethlehem. They could quote chapter and verse to the evil king. And yet these men—the supposed guardians of spiritual truth in Israel—wouldn't bother to walk a few miles south to Bethlehem to find out if the Messiah of Israel had indeed been born.

At least Herod feared Jesus' authority—and tried to nip it in the bud. The innkeeper could claim busyness and ignorance. But what about these men? *They knew better.* They knew the Word of God backward and forward and yet did nothing to respond to it. They were indifferent, too busy with themselves to be concerned about Jesus. In fact, when His public ministry began, they argued with Him and fought Him at every turn. Can you imagine? Arguing with and mocking *God* to His face?

For all practical purposes these were the very men responsible for the execution of Jesus Christ. Why? Because He was a threat to their religious empire. The Bible says that they delivered Him to Pilate because of the envy in their hearts. They envied His authority. They envied the fact that the people loved Him and hung on His every word. They envied that He seemed to have a relationship with God that they lacked.

Addressing this at a later date, Jesus quoted a verse from the prophet Isaiah: "These people honor me with their words while their hearts run far away from me! Their worship is nothing more than a charade!" (Mark 7:6-7, TPT).

They were looking for a different kind of a Messiah, unable to conceive of a Messiah who would suffer and die on a cross for them. They were looking for someone who would support their religious system and their chosen way of living—someone who would cater to their whims and conform to their wishes. Someone who would keep them in power.

There are many people like this today. They want Jesus, but they want Him on their terms.

They want the kind of Jesus they can control.

They want the kind of Jesus who will never challenge them.

They want the kind of Jesus who won't ask them to change their ways.

They want Heaven, but they don't want talk about hell. They want forgiveness, but they are unwilling to repent. They want the imagery of the cross, but they don't want Christ.

I heard a true story about a woman who went into a jewelry store and began looking at various crosses and crucifixes. After examining them for a while, she said to the jeweler, "Do you have any crosses without this little man on them?"

That's how it is for many people today: They want religion, but only for show, according to their own sensibilities. They want truth, but only if it aligns with "their truth."

It's a warning to all of us.

It's possible to get a great many things right in life—the right college, the right career, the right city, the right neighborhood—and miss the most important thing of all.

Thanks and Praise

Dear Lord, thank You for the open doors to serve You and speak for You—and to help and encourage Your people. I don't want to be like the innkeeper and miss a Heaven-sent opportunity because I am distracted or "too busy." Keep me awake and alert, Lord, to how You might use me today.

Back to the Headwaters

"A hope that will never disappoint us."
Romans 5:5, PHILLIPS

I don't know about you, but sometimes I'm ready to be done with it.

Not the celebration of the birth of Jesus, of course, but all of the shallow hoopla of Christmas. I'm talking about the "happy holidays" chatter used to market everything from BMWs to cat food. Sometimes you find yourself wanting to upset the tables of the money changers like Jesus did, but how do you really do that?

Most of us aren't really sick of Christmas; we're sick of what it has become in our culture. But when we set all the noise and accouterments and add-ons aside and just get back into the simple account of our Lord's birth, joy springs up like an artesian well. Getting in a quiet place and reading again the actual account of that night, recorded in the pages of Scripture, is like going back to the headwaters of Christmas.

As I see it, here's our main problem: Many of us try to find joy and happiness in Christmas, when we really need to find our joy and happiness in Christ Himself. And that is a big difference.

When you place your hopes and expectations on a particular celebration or special day on the calendar, you'll find yourself disappointed again and again. But when you place your hopes and expectations on the Lord Himself, He will never, never let you down. As the Scripture says, "This hope will not lead to disappointment. For we know how dearly God loves us, because he has given us the Holy Spirit to fill our hearts with his love" (Romans 5:5, NLT).

The Gospel writer Luke begins the Christmas account with these familiar words:

> *And it came to pass in those days that a decree went out from Caesar Augustus that all the world should be registered. This census first took place while Quirinius was governing Syria. So all went to be registered, everyone to his own city. Joseph also went up from Galilee, out of the city of Nazareth, into Judea, to the city of David, which is called Bethlehem, because he*

was of the house and lineage of David, to be registered with Mary, his betrothed wife, who was with child. (Luke 2:1-5, NKJV)

Dr. Luke reports the facts in meticulous detail. He begins by giving us specific historical information, so we can pinpoint this event in human time.

History tells us that Caesar Augustus was the great nephew of Julius Caesar. A born in-fighter, he had clawed his way into power by defeating Antony and Cleopatra. Then, through considerable genius and force, he gave the Roman Empire a solidity that lasted for centuries. He was the first Caesar to take on the title of "Augustus," which means "of the gods" or "the holy and revered one."

Luke was a stickler for detail. Although he was not one of the twelve disciples nor—as far as we know—an eyewitness of the life and ministry of Jesus, he was the man chosen afterward by the Holy Spirit to put together an accurate account of what Jesus said and did.

In his first chapter, he wrote: "Having carefully investigated everything from the beginning, I also have decided to write an accurate account for you . . . so you can be certain of the truth of everything you were taught" (Luke 1:3-4, NLT).

Like a trained journalist, this physician inter-viewed many of the key players in putting together a precise—and often poetic—account of our Lord's life and work.

In subsequent years, archaeologists have unearthed an inscription dating back to the reign of this Roman ruler. It read: "Augustus Caesar, the savior of the whole world."

That is how this Caesar saw himself . . . which gives Luke 2:11 (NKJV) a whole new dimension of meaning, when the angel says: "There is born to you this day in the city of David a Savior, who is Christ the Lord." Essentially the angel was saying, "Don't look to the palace of Rome for the Savior of the world. Look to the manger in Bethlehem. Don't look at that spoiled, satin-robed, self-proclaimed god in Rome, but look at that humble Baby wrapped in swaddling cloths."

When you really consider the incarnation and life of Jesus, it's not a rags to riches story, it's a riches to rags story. He gave up everything—the unimaginable splendor of Heaven—to serve us and to save us.

On one of the late Queen Elizabeth's visits to the United States, she brought along 5,000 pounds of clothing. (She probably didn't do "carry-on.") Her entourage included two personal valets and her own hairdresser. I read that she even brought her own special leather covers for the toilet seats used by her highness.

That is not traveling light.

Obviously, she didn't leave any of the comforts of home. She brought them all with her so she could continue to live in luxury as head of the royal family.

But look at what Jesus left to come to us and what He gave up. The Bible says that "though he was God, he did not think of equality with God as something to cling to. Instead, he gave up his divine privileges; he took the humble position of a slave and was born as a human being" (Philippians 2:6-7, NLT).

His Story

God moved Caesar Augustus—this little man who was so big in his own eyes—to set forth a decree that everyone should be taxed. Caesar probably congratulated himself on his own good idea to raise the empire's revenue in this way. Caesar thought he was the ultimate king, but in reality, he was just a little pawn on God's chessboard. The *actual* reason for that tax was to get Mary and Joseph to Bethlehem, where the Messiah was prophesied to be born.

It has been said that history swings on the hinge of the door of a stable in Bethlehem. This was the one moment in all of time—"in the fullness of time," as the Scripture says—when God chose to deliver the greatest of all gifts to His rebellious world: the gift of His own Son as Messiah and Savior.

Most of the known world at that time was united under one system of imperial government. Rome had bludgeoned the world into submission, vanquishing all enemies. This forced peace—peace at the point of the sword—became known as *Pax Romana*, "the peace of Rome."

With the absence of war in the civilized world, people could devote more time than usual to pursuits such as literature, art, philosophy, and religion. Greek philosophers like Plato led people into pondering the great imponderables about life, destiny, and human character. As never before, people across the world were probing and searching for meaning.

It could have been a priceless opportunity for God's people, the Jews, to hold high the light of the true and living God. For the most part, however, it was an opportunity lost. If seekers turned to the Judaism of that day, they were bound to be disappointed. Instead of finding a vibrant, living faith as in the glory days of David and Solomon, they would instead find an empty shell, weighted down with innumerable rituals, rules, and regulations that the religious leaders themselves couldn't keep, much less the average man or woman.

Even so . . . there was something in the air.

The rabbis spoke of it.

The poets wrote of it.

Something was stirring. Something was coming.

And it had been a very, very long time coming. Before the angel appeared to Zechariah in the temple foretelling the birth of John the Baptist, there had been 400 years of silence from Heaven. No prophets proclaiming their visions, no angels delivering messages, no miracles to stir people's hearts.

Nothing.

Everything was quiet.

And then everything changed . . . forever.

Thanks and Praise

Praise You, Lord, that Christmas is more than a tradition or custom or day off from work or school. I know that these days of celebration will never feel empty if I am seeking You—Your presence, Your smile, Your counsel in the night—more than anything or anyone else.

DECEMBER 11

Tapping into Peace

"May you know more and more
of grace and peace."
2 Peter 1:2, PHILLIPS

The splendor and magnificence of Heaven came to earth on that night when the angels stepped through the curtain to appear to the shepherds. Though we may never experience an event like that one (on this side of glory), something truly supernatural happens when we worship Jesus Christ. We put our minds on things above and in some way that exceeds our understanding, we actually occupy the same ground as Heaven.

Those aren't just pleasant words to put in a book.

I am talking about something as *real* as sky above and earth below. Listen to how Paul described it to the church at Colosse:

Since you became alive again, so to speak, when Christ arose from the dead, now set your sights on the rich treasures and joys of heaven where he sits beside God in the place of honor and power. Let heaven fill your thoughts; don't spend your time worrying about things down here. (Colossians 3:1-2, TLB)

In other words, set your mind on Jesus Christ and the joys of the next life, and it will affect you in this life.

What, then, was the essence of the angels' message that night to the shepherds?

Don't be Afraid

The angel said, "Don't be afraid."

We read those words, but there is a lot to be afraid of today, isn't there? We're afraid of the future. We're afraid of terrorism. We're afraid of deadly viruses. We're afraid of nuclear war. We're afraid of what's happening in our economy. We're afraid of a runaway artificial intelligence that invades our lives on so many levels. We're afraid of what's going on in popular culture, with twisted values becoming more and more mainstream. We're afraid for our marriages, with all the stresses and strains that seek to tear us apart. We're afraid for the dark world our children and grandchildren will have to navigate.

There is so much to be afraid of. But the angel said, "Don't be afraid."

Did you know that the phrase, "Don't be afraid" is used 365 times in the pages of the Bible? That means that there is one "Don't be afraid" for every day of the year. Fear will always rob us of joy. It's hard to be afraid when you are joyful, and it is hard to be joyful when you are afraid.

A friend recently told me about his experience in a worship service. As the music soared and people around him lifted their hands in praise, the Lord spoke to his heart and said, "You *can't* worship Me. Your insides are completely frozen with fear. Let Me deal with your fear, and then you will be able to praise Me." So he released those fears to the Lord and felt them melt away in that time of worship. And then he could really worship, not just go through the motions.

So . . . "Don't be afraid." And why?

Because the Messiah has Come!

As Scripture says, "A Savior has just been born in David's town, a Savior who is Messiah and Master" (Luke 2:11, MSG).

Why should the shepherds let go of their fear? Because Jesus had come. Messiah had come. And He is the answer to every fear, no matter what it might be.

From our point of view, the Messiah has not only come, He is *coming*. He will return first for His Church, and then to rule and reign on earth and set everything right once again.

Do you ever wonder about your future? *That* is your future: to rule and reign alongside King Jesus forever.

Because Messiah has Come—and will Come Again—REJOICE

"I'm here to announce a great and joyful event that is meant for everybody" (Luke 2:10, MSG)

Ray Stedman said: "The chief mark of the Christian ought to be the absence of fear and the presence of joy." There is so much to be joyful for at this time of year that has nothing whatsoever to do with politics, the economy, the stock market, or what you receive under the Christmas tree.

The key is spending time in God's presence. In the Psalms we're told, "In Your presence is fullness of joy" (Psalm 16:11, NKJV). Another translation reads:

"You have let me experience the joys of life and the exquisite pleasures of your own eternal presence."[10]

And did you know that being joyful is good for your health? We are told in the book of Proverbs, "A happy heart makes the face cheerful, but heartache crushes the spirit." And again, "A cheerful heart is good medicine, but a broken spirit saps a person's strength."[11]

What am I suggesting here? That you walk around with a fake smile plastered on your face saying "praise the Lord" under your breath 24/7? No, I'm not. There is a place for sorrow, mourning, and tears. We can acknowledge our heartaches and disappointments just like anyone else. But underneath it all, like two mighty underground rivers, we can experience joy and hope. And that inner confidence will eventually bubble its way to the surface, even in the darkest of times.

This is such a powerful magnet to the nonbeliever. A Christian who genuinely and authentically rejoices during times of suffering and pain serves as a powerful testimony for Jesus Christ.

Frederick Nietzsche, the atheist and German philosopher once said to some Christians, "If you want me to believe in your Redeemer, you're going to have to look more redeemed." A lot of people don't look redeemed at all; they have a sour disposition—as though they had been baptized in lemon juice, rather than in water. Do you look redeemed?

You might say, "But, Greg, you really don't understand. I'm having a hard time this Christmas. There are problems in my life, problems in my marriage, problems with my kids, problems with my health. My finances are in trouble. My best friend has turned against me. How can I rejoice in Christmas?"

I understand that. But I'm not talking about rejoicing in Christmas. I am talking about rejoicing in Christ. Christ has come. That is how we can have joy.

We have got to get our perspective right. Mankind will *never* bring peace on earth. The United Nations will *never* persuade nations to agree with one another. Politicians will *never* stop plotting new wars—they have been doing it since Eve reached for the forbidden fruit. You can "visualize world peace" all you like, but it will never occur until the Prince of Peace Himself takes His rightful throne. Don't buy into the utopian dream of anybody—any politician, any political philosophy, any political party—bringing peace. We will never see real justice and lasting peace until Christ Himself comes back and establishes His kingdom on earth.

That doesn't mean that we shouldn't hope for peace or work for peace or pray for peace. But it does mean that we need to be realistic in our expectations. As long as human beings are in charge, we will experience friction and conflict.

The promise of Christmas is no promise at all apart from the Christ of Christmas.

He will most certainly bring "peace on earth." But until He does, "We have peace with God because of what Jesus Christ our Lord has done for us. Because of our faith, Christ has brought us into this place of undeserved privilege where we now stand, and we confidently and joyfully look forward to sharing God's glory" (Romans 5:1-2, NLT).

Privilege. Confidence. Joy. Glory.

It doesn't get any better than that.

Thanks and Praise

You are so good and kind to me, Lord. Please let people see Your joy in me today. Not a fakey, plastic joy, but the real thing, bubbling up from Your life in the deepest part of me. Let it shine through my face, my eyes, and my words, touching everyone I meet today.

What We Want and What We Have

"All my longings lie open before you, Lord."
Psalm 38:9, NIV

This Christmas, you may find yourself wishing for a few things that seem out of your reach.

You may be short of resources to give what you would like to loved ones and friends. Ongoing pain might be keeping you on the edge of discouragement and distress, unable to sleep. You may be aching over a broken relationship or slogging through weary weeks of depression. You may be missing a loved one who was with you last year but won't be with you this year.

People on social media seem to have possessions and lives and opportunities and families that you don't.

Life can indeed leave you wishing for more.

But in case you haven't checked your spiritual bank account in a while, let me remind you of the things you *do* have.

You Have a Savior

The Bible says, "There is born to you this day in the city of David a Savior, who is Christ the Lord."[12]

This isn't just history or tradition or happy talk. It is a right-now *reality*. You have a Savior who came to save you from the power and penalty of sin. You were separated from God, and there was nothing you could have ever done to satisfy His righteous demands. Not in a billion years. Not if you could walk across the galaxy for extra credit. But God placed His wrath on Jesus Christ, who died in our place, and when we put our faith in Him, we have the strong assurance we will not die.

Jesus Himself said, "I speak to you this eternal truth: whoever cherishes my words and keeps them will never experience death" (John 8:51, TPT).

Oh yes, our bodies will die and go into the ground (to be resurrected later). But we will live on in eternity. We have God's own guarantee that we will go to Heaven when we leave this earth—because we have a Savior. That's a lot to be thankful for this year.

You Have a Christ

The word *Christ* means "anointed one." Another word that we use is *Messiah*. Jesus was the fulfillment of God's promises to send His Son as the Messiah. It was a reminder to all of us that God keeps His promises.

And what has God promised to you? More than I could relate in this book—or a dozen books. He has promised that you will never be alone. He said, "I will never leave you nor forsake you" (Hebrews 13:5, NKJV). He has promised that He can work all things together for good for those who love Him (Romans 8:28). He has promised He will come again and receive us unto Himself (John 14:3). And He has promised that we will see our loved ones again—in a moment, in the clouds, in the twinkling of an eye (1 Thessalonians 4:17).

You have a Savior. You have a Christ. And finally . . .

You Have a Lord

I'm so glad for this! I can't even tell you how glad. I am no longer in control of my own life. I don't have to be the one to call the shots. I don't have to run around day and night ironing out every little detail. I have a Lord! I have a King! I've never been more aware of that fact than I am now. It's not that I ever thought I really had control in my life; it's just that I have become more acutely aware of how little control I ever had.

The Bible tells us, "A man's heart plans his way, but the LORD directs his steps" (Proverbs 16:9, NKJV). I'm so happy about that. I don't want to be my own tour guide through life. I don't want to direct my own steps because I'll get it wrong every time. I will direct my steps right into a ditch. That's not false modesty; it's completely candid and true. I want God to direct me, even if I don't understand where He's leading me. Even if the road seems dark and difficult.

God is in control of my life, and He is in control of your life as well, if you have put your faith in Christ. He will direct you in the way you should go, and He will protect you and watch over you as you go in that way. And then, when your work is completed, He will welcome you into Heaven, where you will begin a whole new life in a reality a million earthly languages could never describe. That is our hope.

So again (and forgive me for repeating it), don't look to Christmas—the holiday, the square on the calendar—to meet your expectations or fulfill your longings or bring you fulfillment. Look to Christ.

The truth is, we feel let down and disappointed because of false expectations as to what Christmas should be.

Some people don't mind taking time off to commemorate the birth of Jesus, but that's the extent of it. He is all right as long as He stays in that manger as a baby. They don't like the idea of Jesus growing into a man and telling them to turn from their sin and dying on a cross for them and rising again from the dead.

There are many people who say, "I'm OK with God as long as He stays out of my life." They might have a bumper sticker on their car that says, "God is my co-pilot." That's nice. But the fact of the matter is, you shouldn't even be in the cockpit. God doesn't want to be your co-pilot. He wants to be in control of your life.

But that's where people want God. They want Him there when they "break glass in case of emergency," but that's about the extent of their faith. These people wrongly think they make their own luck, that they are the captains of their own ship, the masters of their own destiny.

These are the same people who look down on Christians and say, "You people are a bunch of automatons, marching in lockstep. You want to do the will of God. Well, fine. But I want to do the will of *me*. I'm in control of my own life. I decide what direction I am going to take. My life, my choice. My body, my choice."

I have news for you.

Life doesn't work that way.

People who reject Jesus Christ are *not* in control of their own lives, nor are they making their own luck. According to the Bible, those outside of Christ are under the control of someone else. And that someone else is known as Satan.

In 2 Timothy 2:25–26 (TLB), Paul writes this word to believers: "Be humble when you are trying to teach those who are mixed up concerning the truth. For if you talk meekly and courteously to them, they are more likely, with God's help, to turn away from their wrong ideas and believe what is true. *Then they will come to their senses and escape from Satan's trap of slavery to sin, which he uses to catch them whenever he likes,* and then they can begin doing the will of God" (emphasis mine).

You don't realize this when you're a nonbeliever. You imagine yourself to be in charge of your own life. You convince yourself that you're calling all the shots. You channel Frank Sinatra and sing "I did it *my* way!" But it's strange. Have you ever noticed how most pre-believers all do the same things? They get caught up in the same miserable lifestyle, doing the same tedious things. And then one day, by God's grace, they wake up and look around and say, "What is this? What am I doing here? How did I get to this place? I hate this life."

That's what happened to me, too, as a young man. I started looking around at my life and thought, *This stinks. I'm sick of these stupid parties. I'm tired of drinking and drugs. I can't stand all these cliques and the way these people live. I've had enough of all the backstabbing and hypocrisy. There has to be something better.*

Those thoughts, that inner restlessness and dissatisfaction, sent me on a quest to find purpose and meaning. The adult world that I'd been exposed to certainly wasn't the world where I wanted to live. The empty, unhappy lives of my friends and peers didn't appeal to me either.

So I started looking. My search led me to hearing the gospel and giving my life to Christ. Then I started coming to church, hanging out with God's people, and I began seeing the reality I had been searching for all along. A place where real love and brotherhood and joy could be experienced—not because you were high on something, but through a relationship with God.

Jesus filled all the longings in my life that I had thought could never be filled.

He's still in the business of doing that.

He, and He alone, is the real promise of Christmas.

Thanks and Praise

Thank You, Lord, that I don't have to direct my own steps or stage-manage my own destiny. I'm so relieved and thankful today that my life is in Your hands—through all my years and into the wonders of Heaven. How can I thank You for all Your grace and kindness to me?

Wisdom from the Magi

"We observed a star in the eastern sky
that signaled his birth.
We're on pilgrimage to worship him."
Matthew 2:2, MSG

We know the Christmas card image so well.

There are always three of them, wearing turbans, riding on camels, and silhouetted against a night sky. A huge, magnificent star blazes on the horizon. Tradition has given them names: Gaspar, Melchior, and Balthasar. They even have their own song to sing (in three-part harmony) as they plod along through the sandy wastelands, seeking a new-born king, each wearing his own coordinating color robe and turban:

We three kings of Orient are;
Bearing gifts we traverse afar,

Field and fountain, moor and mountain,
Following yonder star . . .

The Bible, however, never says there were only three, doesn't mention camels, and doesn't give the wise men names.

Let's peel this tradition back and find out who these mysterious men from the East really were, and what they teach us about worship.

The Bible calls them magi. We get our English words *magic* and *magician* from this same term. These were men who consulted the stars and were experts in both astronomy and astrology. Rulers, kings, and pharaohs sought out their counsel and guidance. In contrast to the seers, prophets, and priests of Scripture, the magi used sorcery, wizardry, and witchcraft, combining their science and mathematics with delvings into the occult. Over the years, their religious and political influence continued to grow until they became the most prominent and powerful group of advisors in the Babylonian and Medo-Persian empires.

These magi then, steeped in occultism and false religion, became quite powerful—almost like royalty themselves. They wouldn't have worn the pajama-and-bathrobe kind of outfits (with the pointy shoes) we see depicted on Christmas cards; they would have dressed in a way befitting their status and high office. And they wouldn't have ridden camels; they would have probably entered Jerusalem astride magnificent Arabian stallions. Most likely, a small, mounted army accompanied them for protection. No wonder they created such a stir when that whole resplendent cavalcade rode through the gates of Jerusalem. It was like a foreign army coming in. Most likely, no one had ever seen anything like it.

To top it off, the question they immediately started asking must have swept through the streets like a stiff east wind: *Where is He who is born king of the Jews?* In no time at all, the question went viral.

And here is one more blow to our cherished images: The wise men were not present at the manger in Bethlehem, on the night Jesus was born. Shepherds, yes. Wise men, no. The Bible tells us in Matthew 2:11 that the wise men "came into *the house.*" Not the stable. And when they "saw *the young child*"— not the baby—"with Mary, his mother, they fell to the ground at his feet and worshiped Him" (TPT).

Nevertheless, these wise men from the East knew something that Herod and most others would never know: that this toddler in a tiny, humble house, born to common, working-class people, would one day rule the world. Thus, the magi brought Him gifts befitting a king: gold, frankincense, and myrrh.

Pagan though they may have been, these men understood something else right away: Christmas is about worship.

The religious leaders in Jerusalem knew the Scriptures well enough to point the magi in the right direction in their search for this newborn King: Bethlehem of Judea. But how would they find this one particular child among all the children of that town and that region?

God sent the star ahead of them.

When they heard the king, they departed; and behold, the star which they had seen in the East went before them, till it came and stood over where the young Child was. When they saw the star, they rejoiced with exceedingly great joy. (Matthew 2:9-10, NKJV)

Picture your most joyful moment in life, and then multiply it by ten. These men had traveled a vast distance through desolate and dangerous lands over many weeks, and now they were receiving strong confirmation that they were right on track, and right on schedule. They were going to be granted the privilege of seeing a king whose destiny had somehow been written in the stars.

What did they do when they finally found the house and the young child? They didn't sit on the couch, sip coffee, nibble cookies, and make small talk. They fell down and worshiped Him.

Let me ask you a question. What would make this a perfect Christmas for you? Maybe you're thinking, *If I could just get this one thing I've really been hoping for. . . . I left a detailed map for my parents so they could find the store. . . . I sent a link so my wife could order it online. . . . I put it on my Amazon wishlist as a hint to my husband.*

Or maybe it would be a perfect Christmas for you if your loved one really enjoys the gift you gave, the one you have been scheming about all year. If he or she is truly surprised or touched or excited or blown away . . . ah, that would just make your day.

The trouble is, the events of life rarely live up to our expectations. And Christmas is usually loaded up with all kinds of expectations. We hope the relationship with the in-laws will go better . . . we hope the dinner will come together the way we planned it . . . we hope everyone will get along . . .

we hope that our hearts will just be overflowing with emotions of nostalgia or peace or happiness.

Maybe these things will happen and maybe they won't. But placing our hopes and desires on events turning out a certain way is usually a recipe for a big letdown.

The wise men, however, were particularly wise in the way they celebrated the birth of the King. They worshiped Him. But it wasn't just saying "Merry Christmas" to people on the street or humming "We Three Kings" when they got up in the morning. The Bible says they fell down and worshiped Him. In other words, they gave themselves completely over to praising and adoring the young King. It wasn't a half-hearted, obligatory sort of thing. They planted their faces on the dirt floor because they *wanted* to.

Another translation of verse 11 reads: "They entered the house and saw the child in the arms of Mary, his mother. Overcome, they kneeled and worshiped him."[13]

Immediately afterward, they opened their treasure bags and presented the Child with their precious gifts. Soon after this, God warned them in a dream not to go back through Jerusalem, but to go home a different way. So they were still receiving direction from on high. God was still directing their path.

I have a question for you. Do you think these men went home disappointed? Do you think they left Bethlehem feeling deflated or let down or depressed? Far from it! I think this might have been the crowning event of their whole lives. Through all their years, they would talk about the star, the young King, and the opportunity they had been given to worship Him with all their hearts and offer Him gifts. Will we meet them one day in Heaven? Only God knows, but my guess would be yes.

This is one activity that will never disappoint. Whole-hearted worship of Jesus Christ—giving Him your best, giving Him yourself—will always fill your soul and never deplete it.

Thanks and Praise

Lord and Savior, worship needs to be bigger in my life, I know that. Please keep me from just going through the motions. Keep me from a distracted, half-hearted worship—like checking some box on a "to-do" list. I want to go deeper into thanksgiving and praise than I ever have before.

DECEMBER 14

A Sacrifice of Praise

*"Our constant sacrifice to God
should be lips that give thanks
to his name."*
Hebrews 13:15, PHILLIPS

Herod was lying, of course.

The Bible says that he "called for a private meeting with the wise men, and he learned from them the time when the star first appeared. Then he told them, 'Go to Bethlehem and search carefully for the child. And when you find him, come back and tell me so that I can go and worship him, too!'" (Matthew 2:7-8, NLT).

He didn't want to worship the Christ child at all. He wanted to find that infant King and snuff out His young life. Why? Because this wicked ruler felt that his power might be threatened, and Herod loved power. Actually, he worshiped power. It was the only god he served.

Everyone worships *something* at Christmas.

They may be politically correct and not even utter the word *Christmas*. They may not own a nativity scene or plant an inflated Santa Claus on their front lawn. It doesn't matter. Skeptics worship. Humbugs and grinches worship. Atheists and agnostics worship. Scientists, MMA fighters, and media personalities worship. Conservative Republicans and progressive Democrats and confirmed Independents worship. Even telemarketers worship.

You say, "Greg, I beg to differ with you. Some of those people you mentioned don't worship at all."

But I didn't say they worship *God*. I said they worship. Everyone bows at the altar of something. They may not call it a deity, but they worship something they are committed to and passionate about. Something they believe in. Some people bow at the altar of material things by worshiping their possessions: a car, a house, a bank account, a career, an athletic achievement, a big following on social media. That is their God.

Other people worship their own bodies. They've never met a mirror they didn't love. They spend hours studying the latest diet or sculpting their bodies at the gym or injecting substances into their faces to remove wrinkles. Their own physical appearance is their god.

Other people worship a god of their own making. They say things like this: "Well, *my* god would never judge a person for doing something wrong. *My* god is all-loving and all-caring and all-tolerant." But what god is that? It's certainly not the God of the Bible. In effect, they have created a god in their own image and according to their own notions of right and wrong.

But here is the problem: you can bow at these altars, but none of these gods are able to save you. When the walls close in or the bottom drops out, not one of these gods is going to lift a finger to help. And quite frankly, none of these gods is worthy of your worship. There is only one God worthy of your worship: the living, Triune God—Father, Son, and Holy Spirit.

How, then, do we do it? As Christmas draws near, how do we worship the Lord?

One way is by singing, perhaps some of the great carols of the season. When you're walking through one of the big box stores, you might even be surprised to hear a traditional carol—with a real gospel message—slip in between "Jingle Bells" and "All I Want for Christmas."

> *Then let us all with one accord*
> *Sing praises to our heavenly Lord,*
> *That hath made heaven and earth of nought,*
> *And with his blood our life hath bought . . .*

That's one of the things I love about the Christian faith: We have the best songs! Why is that? Because we have something worth singing about. There is victory and joy and hope and celebration and honor in the songs we sing. What's more, all our singing here is just a warm-up act for eternity. Take a moment to contemplate the awesome scene described in Revelation 5:

> *And every creature which is in Heaven and on the earth*
> *and under the earth and such as are in the sea, and all*
> *that are in them, I heard saying:*

> *"Blessing and honor and glory and power*
> *Be to Him who sits on the throne,*
> *And to the Lamb, forever and ever!"*

> *Then the four living creatures said, "Amen!" And the*
> *twenty-four elders fell down and worshiped Him who*
> *lives forever and ever. (vv. 13-14, NKJV)*

The elders fell down and worshiped the Lord, just as the wise men did at the little house in Bethlehem. And as you and I worship Him with all our hearts, we can enter into that joy that will never, ever fade.

Human beings that we are, however, we don't always feel like praising the Lord. In fact, if the truth were known, it is sometimes the *last* thing we feel like doing. Yet that is the very time when our praise and thanksgiving mean the most. Hebrews 13:15 (NIV) tells us: "Through Jesus, therefore, let us continually offer to God a sacrifice of praise—the fruit of lips that openly profess his name."

When we praise God even when we don't feel like it—when we praise Him through our disappointment or sorrow or tears—we are offering a sacrifice that pleases Him. Think what it means to you when someone you care about gives you a gift or card, looks you in the eyes, and says, "I love you." That expression, if you know it's really from the heart, means more than the gift, doesn't it? In the same way, the Lord likes to hear it when we say to Him, "Lord, I love You" and express that in our worship and our praise.

But that is not the only way we can show our praise and offer our worship to the Lord. Another way is through serving others. Because one of the ways the word *worship* is translated in the Bible is to serve and minister.

We looked at Hebrews 13:15, which speaks about the sacrifice of praise. But the very next verse goes on like this: "And do not forget to do good and to share with others, for with such sacrifices God is pleased" (v. 16, NIV).

The Message translation says it like this: "Make sure you don't take things for granted and go slack in working for the common good; share what you have with others. God takes particular pleasure in acts of worship—a different kind of 'sacrifice'—that take place in kitchen and workplace and on the streets."

Most of us think of worship as what we do when we sing our songs in church, close our eyes, and lift our hands. And indeed, that can be worship. But worship can also be that meal you cook for a sick friend, or that clothing or financial help you provide for someone in need.

I remember when I was in Billy and Ruth Graham's home in North Carolina years ago, before both went to Heaven. Ruth had placed a sign over her kitchen sink that said: "Divine service is conducted here three times a day." It's true. Even washing dishes for your family or friends can be an act of worship.

In John 4:23-24 (NLT), a Samaritan woman wanted to start an argument with Jesus about the best place to worship. Jesus told her, "The time is coming—indeed it's here now—when true worshipers will worship the Father in spirit and in truth. The Father is looking for those who will worship him that way."

In other words, worship isn't about a particular place or a particular time or a particular method. It's about a heart that seeks to connect with God, and that can happen anywhere.

Even in traffic.

Even in busyness and confusion.

Even with an armload of packages and an unhappy toddler.

Even in a lonely prison cell or a windowless room in a rehab center.

Jesus is just as near, just as wonderful as He was for those men from the distant East who found Him in the starlight of Bethlehem.

Thanks and Praise

Father, be with me when things get crazy and busy. Be there in the back of my mind when demands come at me from all sides. Be the song in my heart when I'm tired or fighting through pain or feeling discouraged. Today I declare with the mighty angels who You are and what You have accomplished.

He Comes to Where We Are

"When you come looking for me,
you'll find me."
Jeremiah 29:13, MSG

The wise men, as we have noted, weren't anywhere around on the night when Jesus was born in that stable in Bethlehem. Most likely, they were still back in their observatories in the mysterious East, studying their charts—and perhaps puzzling over the emergence of a strange new star.

The shepherds, however, were eyewitnesses of the events that night—without a doubt the most remarkable night in history, when the Son of God was born to a human mother as a tiny baby. If the birth had happened today, the shepherds would have all had their iPhones out, recording the moment when a million dazzling angels appeared with the good news.

As a group, the shepherds couldn't have been more different than the magi. Where the wise men stood at the top of the economic scale, the shepherds lay at the bottom. In fact, these men were the lowest of the low in Jewish culture.

Jewish society despised and mistrusted shepherds, considering them crafty and dishonest. They didn't allow shepherds to observe the ceremonial hand washings of that day. Nor was the testimony of a shepherd allowed in a court of law. As men of the field, they smelled just like their work: sheep. The only people lower on the social ladder in Israel were lepers.

Think of all the people to whom God might have brought this stunning message. The angels might have easily appeared in the court of Caesar himself. They could have burst into the throne room of King Herod with their glad tidings. The angels could have delivered the announcement to any number of political, military, or economic leaders of the day.

But God didn't send them to the rich, powerful, or influential.

It was as if He had said, "Who are the lowest of the low? Who are the ones that no one cares about?

The shepherds. Those are the ones to whom I will bring My message."

The Lord came to the shepherds where they were, and He came to the magi where they were. So what do we learn from this?

God Comes to Us Wherever We Are

A number of years ago, author Robert McIvor wrote a book titled *Star of Bethlehem, Star of Messiah*. In this book, McIvor cites records from ancient Chinese and Korean astronomers who recorded an unusual star appearing around the time of Christ's birth. In fact, according to the author, the appearance of a mysterious star was a worldwide event. Some scholars think the star may have been an appearance of the Shekinah glory of God.

God specializes in cosmic revelations. After all, He stepped back into human history with angelic appearances to Zechariah, father of John the Baptist; to Mary, the mother of Jesus; and to Joseph, Mary's husband-to-be. Out in the distant East, He began directing the attention of the magi to a mysterious sight in the heavens. And finally, on the night of Jesus' birth, the night sky burst open, with angels unleashing a torrent of praise on a group of frightened shepherds.

The point is, God will come to you wherever you are. No one is beyond His reach.

The shepherds were probably raised in good Jewish homes, where they learned about the God of Israel, the God of Abraham, Isaac, and Jacob. The very sheep they were raising may have been intended for temple sacrifices. If that were the case, they would have been familiar with the need for animal sacrifice to approach God under the old covenant.

You might have been raised in a Christian home, having had the privilege of hearing the Word of God since you were a little boy or a little girl. You have heard the name of Jesus as far back as you can remember.

But sometimes people who have grown up around Christianity all their lives can become more spiritually indifferent than someone who has not been. You might be like some of the religious leaders in Israel at that time—knowing a great many things in your head but without a real relationship with God. You've heard the gospel so many times, and each time you might have said, "Yes, yes, I know all that. I've heard that. I don't want to talk about that."

Don't let that happen to you. Don't let your heart get hardened toward God.

The wise men, on the other hand, were steeped in superstition, occultism, and false belief. God in no way condoned their pagan lifestyle, but He used a star to reach them, draw them, touch their hearts, and bring them to Himself. Wherever you are, God will reach you. Wherever your loved ones are, God can reach them." Many in this age group have wayward children.

As I've mentioned, I wasn't raised in a Christian home, had never heard the Bible, and never went to church. But God invaded my world, and I responded to Him. He can invade yours as well. Anyone who is truly seeking Him will find Him.

That's the starting spot. That's square one on the board of life. *Start looking for God and calling out to Him.* In Jeremiah 29:13 (NKJV), the Lord says, "You will seek Me and find Me, when you search for Me with all your heart." If someone is deceived by a cult or a false belief—as the wise men were—I believe that if they really hunger to know God, He will reveal Himself to them.

That is the story of the whole Bible: It is a record of God revealing Himself to humanity. He is not a

God who hides Himself; He wants men and women to know Him and draw near to Him. In the first chapters of Genesis, what we see is man hiding from God after he had sinned, not God hiding from man. In fact, God came looking for Adam and Eve, calling out, "Where are you?"

In the same way, we as Christians need to go to where people are with the gospel. Jesus didn't say that the whole world should go to church, but He did say that the church should go to the whole world. We need to be like one of those stars, so to speak, that would bring others to Christ. God can use you in that way.

Many follow the latest antics of so-called Hollywood "stars." What are they up to now? What party are they going to? Who is dating whom and who is wearing what? God has zero interest in that. He sees a different kind of star. The person who is a star in God's eyes is the man or woman who will seek to bring others to faith. In fact we are told over in the book of Daniel, "Men and women who have lived wisely and well will shine brilliantly, like the cloudless, star-strewn night skies. And those who put others on the right path to life will glow like stars forever" (Daniel 12:3, MSG).

Did it ever occur to you that you could be a guiding star to someone this Christmas? That's not poetry or hyperbole. What did we just read? "Those who put others on the right path to life will glow like stars forever."

The apostle Paul tells believers in Jesus: "Do everything without complaining or arguing, so that you may become blameless and pure, children of God without fault in a crooked and depraved generation, in which you shine like stars in the universe as you hold out the word of life" (Philippians 2:14-16, NIV1984).

There it is again: *"Shine like stars."*

In other words, "Carry the light-giving Message into the night."[14]

Thanks and Praise

Lord, at this very moment, You see hearts very near despair in places close to me. Let me be a reflection of Your light, Lord, to someone who really needs to see it. I have no light in myself and not much to offer. But I know You can reach out through me to touch someone who needs a little hope.

Waiting for Christmas, (1)

*"In the morning I lay my requests before you
and wait in expectation."*
Psalms 5:3, NIV1984

The apostle James wrote these words: "But let patience have its perfect work, that you may be perfect and complete, lacking nothing."[15]

Those words are in the Bible and I need to listen to them—but I am also calling on the power of God to help me, because I don't like to wait for *anything.*

When I'm in the grocery store and have to check out, I will head straight for the "seven items or less" line—even if I really need to buy more stuff. I'd rather leave the store without the things I want than wait in line. And by the way, I'm carefully counting how many items the person in front of me has placed on the belt, because I don't like cheaters.

Even so, life is full of unavoidable waiting.

As a culture we've become spoiled by instant communication, instant gratification, and instant everything. Can you imagine writing a letter to someone with a really important question, putting it in the mail, and then waiting four or five days—or weeks—for an answer? No, I can't either. (How did people get anything done?) We tend to get upset if someone doesn't respond to our text in a minute and a half.

The pages of the Bible are full of the virtues of waiting (and what happened to people who wouldn't).

Naomi told Ruth, "Wait, my daughter, until you find out what happens. For the man will not rest until the matter is settled today."[16] (She did, and it turned out well.)

Samuel told the young King Saul, "You must wait seven days until I come to you and tell you what you are to do."[17] (He didn't, and it turned out badly.)

In the Psalms David said, "Rest in the LORD, and wait patiently for Him."[18] (And that is always good counsel.)

In the book of Luke, we learn that Simeon waited his whole life for something precious to happen—and it finally did, just a few days after the very first

Christmas. God had revealed to this elderly man that he would not die until he saw the Messiah with his own eyes. What a promise!

Sometimes Christmas gifts arrive early from people who live out of state. And they are usually marked with the words, "Do not open until Christmas!" You just have to wait—even when they arrive a month early.

God's marching orders to Simeon went like this: "Stay alive! And keep your eyes open. If you do, you will see the Messiah!"

Four hundred years before the birth of Jesus, the prophet Malachi had captured these words from the Lord: "But to you who fear My name the Sun of Righteousness shall arise with healing in His wings" (Malachi 4:2, NKJV). And like many of the faithful among God's people, Simeon had looked and longed for that event through all of his days. Then, when he was very old, just when he thought he might not live to see it, God's Spirit whispered "that he would not see death before he had seen the Lord's Christ" (Luke 2:26, NKJV).

So here was Simeon, waiting for Christmas or, more specifically, waiting for Christ. Had he heard about the birth in Bethlehem, just a few days before, just a few miles away? Had he heard the rumors of excited shepherds and choirs of angels? The Bible doesn't say. But Luke does tell us that on one momentous morning, the Holy Spirit led His elderly servant into the temple courts.

Do you think he was glad he made that decision? There's no question!

Have you ever thought about not going to church on a certain Sunday morning and then, at the last minute, decided to go? Perhaps when it was over, you found yourself saying, "I'm so glad I was in God's house with God's people today. The Lord really had something special for me."

That's how Simeon would have felt—times a million. Because as he entered the temple courts, he bumped into a young couple carrying a little baby.

And Simeon knew immediately. *This is the One. This is God's Messiah. This is the Desire of all Nations.*[19]

How did he know? Did Mary and Joseph and the baby have little halos around their heads like you see on Christmas cards? Did they glow as they walked through the corridors? No, there wouldn't have been any halos. To all outward appearances, this was just a common laborer with a young wife, tenderly carrying a newborn.

Simeon would have seen right away that they were impoverished. They were holding two doves as a sacrifice, which was God's provision for people who couldn't afford anything else. But Simeon had no hesitation. The Spirit had told him, "There He is!"

Walking right up to Mary and Joseph, he took the baby into his arms and began to praise God.

> "Lord, now You are letting Your servant
>   depart in peace,
> According to Your word;
> For my eyes have seen Your salvation
> Which You have prepared before the face of
>   all peoples,
> A light to bring revelation to the Gentiles,
> And the glory of Your people Israel."
> (Luke 2:29-32, NKJV)

Mary and Joseph, of course, were stunned by this event. And then the old man turned to Mary with a personal message. Looking into her eyes with what must have been a strange intensity, he said: "This child is destined to cause many in Israel to fall, and many others to rise. He has been sent as a sign from God, but many will oppose him. As a result, the deepest thoughts of many hearts will be revealed. And a sword will pierce your very soul" (Luke 2:34-35, NLT).

Simeon, whose name means "God has heard," had been waiting and waiting for that very moment. He waited with faith. He waited with expectation. The Bible says, "He was righteous and devout and was eagerly waiting for the Messiah to come and rescue Israel. The Holy Spirit was upon him" (2:25, NLT).

Those words "eagerly waiting" could be translated *alert to His appearance.*

Sometimes people will say, "I never hear from God." And I want to reply, "Are you eagerly waiting? Are you eagerly listening? Are you taking time to be with Him?"

I think the reason many of us don't hear from God is because we haven't bothered to tune in to His frequency. We aren't finding a quiet place or a quiet moment to seek Him out.

Here's a radical thought. Ready?

If you want to hear from God, put down your cell phone. Turn off the tablet. Turn off the TV. Turn off the music. Take a walk on the beach or go outside with a Bible in your lap, read a little, and listen for His voice. If you don't live in sunny Southern California, bundle up and go for a walk or sit by the fire in a quiet room.

Simeon was eagerly waiting for Jesus to come the first time—and He did.

But guess what? Jesus will also come a second time. He will come in the twinkling of an eye for His Church, calling us into the clouds. And after that, He will come leading a mighty army of angels and God's people to rule and reign on earth.

I can't even describe how exciting that is.

That's something to wait and watch for every day of our lives.

Hebrews 9:28 (NLT) says, "He will come again, not to deal with our sins, but to bring salvation to all who are eagerly waiting for him." There it is again. Eagerly waiting!

Are you eagerly awaiting the return of Christ? I think that is a real test to determine where you are spiritually. If you are right with God, you will long for the return of Christ. If you are not right with the Lord, or perhaps living in a way you should not be living, you may find yourself dreading His return—or worse, becoming apathetic about it.

The first time He came to a manger. Next time He'll come in glory.

The first time he came in swaddling clothes. Next time He'll come in a robe dipped in blood.

The first time He was surrounded by shepherds and animals. The next time He will be accompanied by saints and angels.

The first time there was no room in the inn. The next time the door of the cosmos will swing open wide for Him.

The first time He came as the Lamb of God who would die for the sins of the world. The next time He will return as the ferocious Lion of the tribe of Judah.

Yes, He is coming back, and like Simeon, we should live in anticipation of that day.

This is something infinitely worth waiting for.

Thanks and Praise

Lord, it's been too long since I thought about Your return—what it will be like and when it might happen. Help me to live like Simeon, leaning hard on Your promise, listening for Your voice, and realizing that the next person coming around the corner might be Jesus Messiah.

Waiting for Christmas, (2)

*"She also began thanking God
and telling everyone in Jerusalem . . .
that the Messiah had finally arrived."*
Luke 2:38, *TLB*

Eight days after Jesus was born, Mary and Joseph took Him into the temple to have him circumcised, according to the law of Moses. That's where they encountered Simeon, a godly old man who had been eagerly waiting for the Messiah.

That was an unforgettable encounter for this young couple. Scripture says that Mary and Joseph "marveled" over how this total stranger had somehow recognized their baby, and what he had spoken over Him. Another translation says that "Jesus' father and mother were speechless with surprise at these words."[20]

But they had hardly a moment to recover from that meeting before someone else walked around the corner. This time, an elderly woman approached with wonder in her eyes. Here's how Dr. Luke captures the scene:

> Anna, a prophet, was also there in the Temple. She was the daughter of Phanuel from the tribe of Asher, and she was very old. Her husband died when they had been married only seven years. Then she lived as a widow to the age of eighty-four. She never left the Temple but stayed there day and night, worshiping God with fasting and prayer. She came along just as Simeon was talking with Mary and Joseph, and she began praising God. She talked about the child to everyone who had been waiting expectantly for God to rescue Jerusalem. (Luke 2:36-38, NLT)

Can you visualize this moment? Simeon had just looked into Mary's eyes and, speaking of her son's future, had said, "Many will oppose him. As a result, the deepest thoughts of many hearts will be revealed. *And a sword will pierce your very soul.*"[21]

As Mary was trying to digest these sobering words, a grandmotherly woman walked around the corner, saw them, and immediately began praising

God out loud! I have a feeling that didn't happen often in those temple corridors.

Anna had been a widow most of her life, losing her husband early. For all practical purposes, she had lived in the temple most of her life.

How did she live? How did she get by or provide for herself? Was she known among the godly in Jerusalem as a prophetess? The Bible doesn't say. And these few lines in the book of Luke are all we know of her. But through the millennia, her life has been linked to Mary and Joseph, to Jesus, and to the Christmas story.

Scripture says, "She talked about the child to everyone who had been waiting expectantly for God to rescue Jerusalem." Another translation puts it like this: "From that day forward she told everyone in Jerusalem who was waiting for their redemption that the anticipated Messiah had come!"[22]

She became an elderly evangelist! And she spread the word about Jesus to those who had been waiting and watching for Messiah, just as she and Simeon had.

Even in these few verses, Anna shows us how a believer should live.

What did she do? She did the four things we counsel all new believers to do. When someone indicates a desire to accept Jesus as Savior, our church lays out four simple things. We tell brand-new Christians that they need to study God's Word every day, to pray, to be part of the church, and to share their faith.

That's exactly what Anna did. Here is a woman who studied God's Word—and must have known all the Messianic prophecies in Scripture by heart. She worshiped and fasted, she went to church (or in her case, the temple), and she enthusiastically shared Jesus with others.

Anna and Simeon were both up in years; their objective was to stay alive until Christmas—that is, until their eyes rested on the Christ of Christmas.

Simeon held hope in his arms when he held Jesus, and he died with that hope. Hope has a name, and it is Jesus. Simeon held on to that hope. And Anna apparently went out to the streets and spread that hope all over town.

We have that same hope of life after death.

Speaking of death at this time of year might seem like a downer to some, but the truth is, Christmas and death are inseparably connected. Don't forget that the angel said to Joseph of Jesus, "He will save His people from their sins" (Matthew 1:21, NIV). And when the wise men came later, one of their gifts—myrrh—was an embalming element. Somehow they knew that the life and death of this newborn King were inextricably linked. He was born to die for a purpose.

Late in His ministry, Jesus knew that His own disciples still didn't grasp His mission. On one occasion, after breaking up an argument among them, Jesus said, "The Son of Man came not to be served but to serve others and to give his life as a ransom for many" (Matthew 20:28, NLT).

He came to us that first Christmas, and it remains the most joyful event in all history. But He came to die and to give His life as a ransom—because we are all sinners and need a Savior.

But even knowing our need, it's hard for us to jump into His open arms.

I remember the time when I was in my house, watching something on TV, and I distinctly heard the voice of my wife, Cathe, saying, "Greg!"

I looked around the house, going from room to room, but she wasn't there. I looked out the front window and a back window but couldn't see her. So I thought maybe I had imagined it and went back to my TV program.

Then I heard it again. She was yelling my name even louder.

I went out the front door and she wasn't there. I walked around to the backyard and there she was: up in a tree! I looked up at her said, "Umm, why are you up in a tree?"

The reason was a little complicated.

It seems she was carrying out some trash (it should have been me) and got locked into a little walled space adjacent to the garage. The doors to the garage and that enclosed area were both locked. Resourceful lady that she is, she climbed up on the trash can, got into the branches of an overhanging tree, and then couldn't get down from the tree.

So she was yelling, "Greg, help me!"

I looked up and said, "Jump into my arms! I'll catch you." (I was trying to be Prince Charming, I guess.)

And she said, "No way. Get a ladder."

I don't think she fully trusted that I wouldn't drop her. So I got the ladder for her, she got down safely, and that ended our little adventure.

It was different with the grandkids when they were little. They would leap into my arms from chairs or tables or countertops without a moment's hesitation. Sometimes they didn't even tell me they were coming; they just flung themselves at me and I caught them at the last second.

Sometimes in life we can get stuck in some pretty uncomfortable or even scary places. Maybe it's a health issue, or a financial crisis, or a relationship that's falling apart. And the Lord says, "Here I am. Jump into My arms!"

But we're not always ready to trust Him, are we? We're not ready to surrender, let go, and release everything to Him. Maybe some are not willing to trust Him for salvation.

We can trust the Redeemer to catch us.

We can trust the Savior and mighty Son of God to hold us.

We can trust Him to take us to Heaven, and we can trust Him with our most difficult dilemmas and anxieties here on earth.

That's why He came.

Thanks and Praise

Thank You for this account, Lord, of a lady who spoke of her hope every day. It's so easy to fall into negative or cynical remarks that don't help anyone and don't change a thing. As best as I know how, I surrender my words to Your Spirit today. I want to speak out my hope, not my doubts or my fears.

Conflict and Peace

"Do you think I came to smooth things over
and make everything nice?
Not so. I've come to disrupt and confront!"
Luke 12:51, MSG

This may come as a shock to you, but Christmas, at its essence, is not about love, peace, harmony, and sipping hot cocoa with family around a crackling fire. It's not about Currier and Ives depictions of horse-drawn sleighs, snowmen with top hats, and rosy-cheeked people wearing red scarves.

Christmas is actually about conflict. It always has been and always will be.

In the book of Revelation, we find a passage that unexpectedly deals with the subject of Christmas—but you will probably never find it depicted on a Christmas card. In this passage, a pregnant woman is being pursued by a powerful dragon who seeks her death. As she begins to give birth, the dragon hovers over her, waiting to destroy the child.

The woman is a picture of Israel, the child is Jesus Christ, and the dragon is Satan.

This is Christmas from a heavenly perspective. And it gives us the big picture of what was happening when God sent His Son into the world. Satan opposed it—remembering all too well the prophetic word to Eve in the Garden of Eden (Genesis 3:15). And we can see how this great struggle is still in play today.

Hostility toward Christmas and Christians seems to escalate a little more every year. More nativity scenes are being removed from public spaces, and Christmas carols are simply not allowed in some places. Meanwhile, atheists put up vile billboards attacking the Christian faith. And many would rather say the generic greeting, "Happy holidays" than utter the word *Christmas*. These are all symptoms of the conflict of Christmas.

As I have often said, the most intolerant people in the world are those who talk most about "tolerance." Christians, for the most part, are very tolerant. Every day I see or hear things on television, the radio, or even on freeway billboards that offend me. But I don't burn down the billboards or try to get people fired from the television shows who say things I don't like. I tolerate it. And I expect the same from others because we still live in a country where we can express our views freely.

Although I don't agree with certain views, I do support someone's right to state his or her views. And I expect the same for my point of view. That is one of the beautiful things about our country.

There are people today, however—and their tribe is increasing—who don't want us to merely tolerate their views. They want us to accept them and actually *endorse* them—even when they directly violate the clear teaching of Scripture.

This simply cannot happen. Because as Christians, we *stand* on Scripture, the unchanging and eternal Word of God.

Someone might say, "Can't we just set all the unpleasantries and disagreements aside and embrace the peace and love of the season?"

Truthfully, we can't.

Jesus did not come to bring a mind-numbing "peace on earth" devoid of truth. The angels did not distribute Prozac when their appearance cut through the night sky, ripping open the heavens with light rushing across the fields like water from a broken levee.

Their message to the shepherds on the night of Christ's birth was, "Glory to God in the highest, and on earth peace, goodwill toward men!"[23] Another translation puts it this way: "Glory to God in highest Heaven, and peace on earth *to those with whom God is pleased*."[24] In other words, the only way we will have peace on earth is when we are pleasing to God.

The Battle We Face

Jesus made a rather provocative statement in Luke 12:51 (NKJV): "Do you suppose that I came to give peace on earth? I tell you, not at all, but rather division." This is the division between light and darkness, righteousness and unrighteousness, good and evil, right and wrong, and yes, Christ and Antichrist.

What we are seeing played out in our culture is a battle between the God of the Bible—the true and living God—and all contenders. This warfare is nothing new. It goes all the way back to the Garden of Eden. After Satan temped Adam and Eve and they fell, God said to the serpent: "And I will cause hostility between you and the woman, and between your offspring and her offspring. He will strike your head, and you will strike his heel" (Genesis 3:15, NLT).

Here is the same verse in a paraphrase: "I'm declaring war between you and the Woman, between your offspring and hers. He'll wound your head, you'll wound his heel."[25]

Red is the color of Christmas. But that isn't because it's the color of Santa Claus's suit or our favorite decorations or gift wrap. No, red is the color of Christmas because of the blood of Jesus Christ that would be shed. The cradle pointed to the cross. The birth of Jesus pointed to the death of Jesus.

As we have already seen, even in the earliest days of our Lord's infancy, Simeon prophesied to His mother, Mary, "He has been sent as a sign from God, but many will oppose him. As a result, the deepest thoughts of many hearts will be revealed. And a sword will pierce your very soul."[26]

Mary's heart must have been singing over the birth of Jesus. But this was a sharp reminder that His birth signaled great conflict for years—and centuries—to come. And as events played out in Mary's own lifetime, her heart would be broken.

As we have seen, Matthew's Gospel gives an account of the coming of the wise men from the East. Their arrival in Jerusalem, seeking the one born "King of the Jews," introduces us to one of the worst villains of the Bible: King Herod. History calls him "Herod the Great." He was raised in a politically well-connected family, destined for a life of hardball and power brokering. He was the consummate corrupt politician.

By age 25, he was named governor of Galilee, and the Romans hoped he could control the Jews under his authority. In 40 B.C., the Roman Senate gave him the title "King of the Jews," of which he was very proud.

Herod was addicted to power and known for his cruelty. Anyone whom he perceived as a threat he quickly eliminated. Human life meant nothing to him.

So when the magi came riding into town asking for the King of the Jews, they created quite a stir. There wasn't a worse thing anyone could have said to this evil ruler. And when he realized that the wise men wouldn't be reporting back to him with the location of the child, he was furious. That's when he gave the unthinkable command to put to death all the boys under age two in Bethlehem.

Herod, the man who tried so hard to stop Christmas, came to complete ruin. In the final year of his life, he was in so much pain from disease that he screamed through the night. He ended up on the ash heap of history like so many other dictators before and after him.

People who live wicked lives will eventually reap what they sow. And all who blaspheme God, fight with God, or try to stop the work of God will eventually fail. But God's Word will prevail.

Even though we savor the holiday with all its lights and beauty and food and cherished traditions, we who love the Lord Jesus might remember that the day also marks a great conflict. The enemy did not want Jesus to be born in Bethlehem. He did not want the Son of God to walk this earth and bring words of life to all people. And He especially didn't want Him to give His life as a blood sacrifice for the sins of humanity, so that we might escape Satan's grip and find salvation and eternal life.

When you hear people in our culture seeking to cancel Christmas or hide the name of Jesus from public view, remember to be awake and alert and aware, keeping your walk with Him fresh and new.

There really is peace on earth, even in the middle of noise and conflict. And it is in the hearts of men and women and boys and girls who daily follow Jesus as Lord.

Thanks and Praise

Jesus, Your birth was a victory over Satan. He didn't want You to come. He didn't want "God with us" or anywhere near us! He didn't want me to be redeemed. Praise You, Lord, for breaking through the darkness and coming to us as a vulnerable infant—and for growing up to be my Redeemer and Friend.

What about Happiness?

"I have told you these things
so that you will be filled with my joy."
John 15:11, NLT

"*It's the most wonderful time of the year . . .*
It's the hap-happiest season of all . . ."

We've heard those lyrics, of course, at least a thousand times. But it doesn't always help us to be happy just because we are *supposed* to be happy.

People expect to be happy and joyful in the Christmas season—like families in the old movies or on the Hallmark Channel. But it doesn't always work that way. Flipping the calendar to December doesn't flip a switch that changes your outlook or circumstances. Maybe you're going through some deep waters right now and it's a difficult time for you. Maybe you're missing someone who is far away or has passed on. It's hard for you to identify with "Good tidings of great joy"—even if they were delivered by those long-ago angels.

Christmas can be a sad and unhappy time for many. You look at people celebrating all around you and you feel left out. Or you peruse social media and see what seem to be ideal marriages and families, and you wonder what happened to yours.

We all need to get back to the original idea of what Christmas is all about.

And it is about joy—in spite of our circumstances.

Why? Because a Savior has been born.

The shepherds heard an angel say to them, "I bring you good tidings of great joy." Not just joy, but *great* joy. In essence, the angel was telling these men on the night shift, "Go ahead and rejoice *whether you feel like it or not*, because your world has just changed forever!"

And did you know that having the joy of the Lord is one of the most powerful magnets in your life for the gospel? It is a high-impact moment when Christians can reflect a calm and joyful spirit in the midst of setbacks, heartaches, and adversity.

David wrote "Restore to me the joy of Your salvation, and uphold me by Your generous Spirit. Then I will teach transgressors Your ways, and sinners shall be converted to You" (Psalm 51:12-13, NKJV). Notice the connection David makes between the joy of his salvation and sinners being converted.

Remember the account of Paul and Silas, who were thrown into a dungeon in Philippi for preaching the gospel?[27] First, they were savagely beaten. Then they were put into chains and stocks. Their backs bled freely, their muscles cramped from the stocks, and their prospects didn't look good. Humanly speaking, there wasn't much hope of them ever getting out.

But when we talk about the truths of the Bible, it's a lot more than "humanly speaking." With God, there is always hope. The book of Acts tells us, "Around midnight Paul and Silas were praying and singing hymns to God, and the other prisoners were listening."[28]

That's an interesting phrase: "the other prisoners were listening." It could better be translated, *"They were listening with pleasure."* They leaned forward in their chains. They had never heard anything quite like this.

It wasn't what Paul and Silas were singing or how they were singing. It was *where they were* when they sang.

Then an earthquake came, so violent that it shook the foundations of the prison. Chains fell off the prisoners' hands and legs, and the doors flew open.

The Roman jailer knew that if those prisoners escaped, he would forfeit his own life. In despair, he thought he might as well get it over with and commit suicide on the spot. But no one had escaped! Paul and Silas called out to the jailer, and said, "Don't kill yourself! We are all here."

Trembling with emotions, the jailer said, "Sirs, what must I do to be saved?" In other words, "I've been watching you guys, and I want what you have. I need it right now." It's because they were able to rejoice even when times were hard.

The jailer had been given an order by the city magistrates to throw these guys into super-max confinement. And if it had been dark in the main part of the prison, this place was *really* dark. Paul and Silas probably couldn't even see each other in that inky blackness.

Researchers tell us that people's outlook on life can be affected by a lack of light. And because December is the shortest and darkest month of the year, people may experience a condition called "seasonal affective disorder," or SAD. But here were two disciples of Jesus in what may have been the darkest place of the city, singing to God for all they were worth.

And their joy in the Lord went right through the walls, so that the other prisoners heard it and marveled at it. Paul and Silas couldn't move, couldn't escape, and probably couldn't even see. But their song of joy in Jesus went viral from one end of the prison to the other.

This sort of response draws attention. It's powerful.

When you think about it, nonbelievers have nothing like it. Sure, they have their occasions of happiness, but those moments come and go. And take note of this: *Their happiness is completely dependent on their circumstances.* But the joy that we experience in Christ can be ours whether we are in good times or bad.

That isn't natural. It's supernatural. And that's what turns heads and hearts.

Happiness and joy are certainly ours to experience . . . at Christmas and always. But it's not a mere holiday or a particular numbered square on a calendar that will lift our hearts.

The joy comes to us as a living Person.

And one final thing from the angels' message in Luke 2:11: "There is born to you *this day* in the city of David a Savior" (NKJV).

This day.

We might think, "I'll be happy tomorrow. I'll breathe easier next week when my grades come in or when my next paycheck arrives, because I'm overextended. I'll be happy and joyful when I see what I get for Christmas, or when I finally get through this present trial. Then I'll be able to smile again."

Not necessarily!

After you come out of the trial you are in now, there will be another one around the corner, perhaps sooner rather than later. That's not pessimism, that's reality on Planet Earth.

Ray Steadman wrote: "A Christian is one who is completely fearless, continually cheerful, and constantly in trouble." It's always going to be something. Don't you know that by now? If you're not going through some kind of difficulty, either you are not breathing or you are in major denial. We all have problems in life. Don't feel like you're the exception. *But rejoice anyway.*

You say, "I'll rejoice when I get through this situation." No. Rejoice when you are *in* the situation. In fact, you are commanded to do so. In Philippians 4:4, the apostle Paul says, "Rejoice in the Lord always. Again I say, rejoice!" (NKJV). In the original language, it's neither a suggestion nor a pleasant devotional thought.

It's a command.

By the way, when Paul penned those words, he wasn't lying on some beach sipping an iced tea with a tiny umbrella in the glass. He was a man in a Roman prison awaiting news of his fate.

But even amid such bleak circumstances, Paul says to the Philippians (and all of us), "I have a message for you: *Lighten up!* Rejoice in the Lord always." In other words, "If anyone has reason to be depressed, it is me. But I am *not* depressed. And you don't have to be either."

If you are looking to this world to make you happy, you never will be. If you are looking to your husband or wife or friends or grandchildren to make you happy, you never will be. If you are looking to Christmas to make you happy, you never will be.

Only the Lord Jesus can do that, and He can start this very day.

Turn to Him.

Thanks and Praise

Dear Lord, right now I look to You to refresh my soul and spirit. Wash away the worries, anxieties, fears, and negative thoughts, and forgive all my sins. I can't change my own outlook or mood, but Your Spirit can change me—from the inside out. Let Your life flow through me now like a sweet, clean wind.

DECEMBER 20

Keeping Him in View

"I have set the LORD always before me."
Psalm 16:8, NKJV

It's a sad fact of the times we live in but true: Many people this time of year work feverishly to remove any remembrance of Jesus from public view.

In Portland, Maine, a site manager for that city's housing authority recently attempted to clarify a new policy banning all religious celebrations or decorations, stating: "There shall be no angels, crosses, stars of David or any other icons of religion displayed on the walls, floors, ceilings, etcetera up on your apartment buildings except within your own apartment."

The dictum went on to decree that anything hanging on the inside of the resident's door was permissible, but nothing whatsoever was allowed on the outside, exposed to the hallway, because "it might offend someone."

Or how about the grade school principal in Sacramento, California, who strictly warned his teachers against including the word *Christmas* on any written materials within their classrooms.

As I've already mentioned, I refuse to say "happy holidays" to anyone.

My recommendation? Say "Merry Christmas" to people—cheerfully, distinctly, politely, and without shame! Or when you receive one of those wimpy "happy holidays" greetings, smile your brightest smile and say, "Why thank you! And God bless you," or "Jesus loves you." We who belong to Jesus ought to have no shame in declaring His name or His love. We *own* Him in public, just as He owns us.

The attempt to remove every vestige of Christmas, has gone to almost-unbelievable lengths. Now even the humble *snowflake* has been deemed offensive. In Saratoga Springs, New York, third graders at Division Street Elementary School saw their Christmas project confiscated by an indignant principal. Entering their classroom, he was struck with horror when he saw the boys and girls adorning an oversized Christmas ornament with colored photos of snowflakes. He quickly removed the offending item from sight, and there is no word as to whether the teacher was allowed to keep her job. (She probably had to attend sensitivity training.)

Others have banned poinsettias for alleged "religious connotations." All of this seems incredibly overreactive and sad to me.

But when you think about it, there's something even more sad than that: when sincere believers in the Lord Jesus Christ simply lose sight of Him during the very season set apart to honor His entry into our world.

Missing Person

Did you ever feel as though you somehow lost God from your life? One day as you were going about your affairs, you suddenly realized that something seemed missing. And that's when it dawned on you that you hadn't given a single thought to God all day—or maybe for several days. That connection with Heaven you had always enjoyed seemed distant.

It was almost as though He were gone.

We can lose God in the holiday season—and it's really not that hard to do.

The book of Hebrews tells us: "This is why it is so crucial that we be all the more engaged and attentive to the truths we have heard so that we do not drift off course" (Hebrews 2:1, TPT).

That word *drift* is interesting. We drift from God like a boat that has lost its moorings; but He doesn't drift from us. If you feel far from God, *guess who moved?* God hasn't gone anywhere, but maybe *we* have. And in the busyness of the season and the so-called celebration of the birth of Christ, we can forget all about Him.

You know how it is. On Wednesday there's a "white elephant" party at the office. Then on Thursday, there's that special Christmas movie you wanted to see with the family. And the weekend? Yikes! You haven't sent Christmas cards yet . . . and there's so much shopping, how will you ever get it all done?

Somewhere in it all we lose track of our Lord.

Maybe there was a point in your life where you walked closely with the Lord, but in recent days it seems like you've lost sight of Him.

I'm reminded of the words of Jesus to the church of Ephesus in Revelation 2, when He says, "I know your deeds, your hard work and your perseverance. . . Yet I hold this against you: You have forsaken your first love. Remember the height from which you have fallen! Repent and do the things you did at first. If you do not repent, I will come to you and remove your lampstand from its place" (Revelation 2:2, 4-5, NIV1984).

From this account, the First Church of Ephesus seemed a busy, active, productive congregation. They wouldn't tolerate false teaching, and they seemed to have all their doctrinal ducks in a row.

But somehow, in all that activity, work, and study, they had lost sight of Jesus. And the Lord Himself had to say to them, "You have left your first love."

Work had taken the place of worship. Perspiration had taken the place of inspiration. Programs had taken the place of passion. So the Great Physician, our Lord Himself, wrote them a prescription for renewal or revival: *Remember from where you have fallen. Repent and do the first works quickly.* I sum it up like this: There are three Rs of getting right with God. Remember. Repent. Repeat.

So maybe there was a time when you felt closer to God, but now, for whatever reason, you're not in that place. You can remember what it was like. You read one of your old journals and it seems to just overflow with love for Jesus. But now there's a distance.

What do you do? It's not rocket science! Remember where you were and go back to that place.

Do you remember the way it was when you first came to Jesus Christ? Do you remember the passion, the excitement?

Remember from where you have fallen.

Repent and change your direction.

Repeat, doing those things you used to do when Jesus was number one in your life.

Have you lost sight of Jesus this Christmas season? As we enter a new year let's make a real effort to remember Him by taking time for the Word of God. And by that, I mean carving out time for Bible study. Don't just try to work it into your busy schedule. *Change* your busy schedule and make time for God's Word.

Let's remember Him by taking time each and every day for prayer—a time to spend in the presence of God, listening to His voice as well as baring your heart to Him and bringing your petitions to Him. In Luke 18:1 (NLT) we read that "Jesus told his disciples a story to show that they should always pray and never give up."

Let's remember Him in our involvement in church, with His people. Not just working it in when you can find time, but understanding that there is a priority in gathering with God's people for worship and prayer. Church is not just a place where we take in. It is also a place where we give out. It is a place to use the gifts God has given to us, seek spiritual accountability, and listen to the advice others give to us. It is a place to invest our finances and share in what God is doing.

Remember Him also as you look for opportunities to share your faith with others. The Christmas season is such a natural time to speak about Jesus, to tell others about this One who has been born and was crucified and has risen again from the dead.

Celebrating Christmas—with enthusiasm, laughter, reverence, and great joy—is a wonderful tradition.

But keeping Jesus in view through the hours of the day is life itself.

Thanks and Praise

Lord, in Your Word You say that You are "thinking about me constantly,"[29] but I have trouble just keeping You in view sometimes. I get distracted or caught up in a thousand racing thoughts. I ask today that You would remind me of Your presence and keep me close to You. I don't want to drift from Your love.

DECEMBER 21

Blue Collar Foster Dad

"Joseph was a righteous man
full of integrity."
Matthew 1:19, TPT

Everyone talks about Mary's place in the Christmas story. We honor Mary, as we should, and she is the one who appears in so many Christmas songs and carols.

But what about Joseph?

We sing, "Mary, Did You Know?" but we don't sing, "Joseph, did you know?" We love "The Little Drummer Boy" and how he played his *pa-rum-pum-pum-pum* drum solo. Mary nodded and the baby smiled, the song tells us, but where was Joseph?

Other than a detailed genealogy in Matthew 1, we really don't know much about Joseph. We know that he was a direct descendant of King David, that he had a carpenter shop in Nazareth, and that he and Mary had other children besides Jesus.[30] Yet he never spoke one recorded word in Scripture, and he disappeared from the pages of the Bible after Luke chapter 2, when he and Mary lost track of twelve-year-old Jesus in Jerusalem.

Even though not much is said about Joseph, he certainly isn't a minor player in the story of Jesus. Just as surely as God chose Mary to be the mother of the Messiah, God handpicked Joseph to be the father figure on earth for Jesus. Think of it. Out of all the men on earth in all of time—including kings and princes and rulers and scholars—our almighty heavenly Father picked out *this* man to raise the Son of God.

A blue-collar guy. Joseph was a skilled craftsman whose own father probably taught him the trade. I think God must have said, "I want a man's man to raise My Son. I want a man with callouses on his hands who knows how to put his back to a task. I want a man with personal integrity."

As a carpenter, Joseph chopped down trees, framed houses, and built furniture. He was no doubt a strong man with broad shoulders who put in long days and took pride in his work. And that's the example God wanted for Jesus as He grew up.

The Bible doesn't tell us what happened to Joseph after he disappeared from Scripture. We read of Mary, who was there throughout the life of Jesus, right up to the end—to the day of Pentecost and the coming of the Holy Spirit. We know that she eventually moved in with the apostle John, who looked after her.

But what happened to Joseph? Did he die in the arms of Mary and Jesus? That would be a happy thought, but the Bible has no record of it. Joseph must have died as Jesus was growing up, but however long his life may have been, he was a godly and selfless man. How do we know that? Think back to a certain moment after he and Mary became engaged.

She had experienced the visit from Gabriel and then the first unmistakable signs of pregnancy. She knew very well that she had been virtuous and that she was now pregnant. How do you break that news to your fiancé? Think what it would have been like for *him*. Mary comes to him and says, "Joseph, honey, I know we're getting married soon, but I have some news for you. I'm pregnant."

What was the man to think? Obviously, that Mary had become involved with another man and that she was carrying that man's child. So in his mind, the engagement and marriage were off. How could it be otherwise?

Mary would have gone on to say—probably with tears, "You don't understand, Joseph. This is from the Holy Spirit! I am the fulfillment of a prophecy." And Joseph may have slowly shaken his head and thought, *Yeah, right.*

But because he was a good man—and I'm sure he truly loved Mary—he didn't want to humiliate or disgrace her. So he thought, *I'll just do this quietly and move on. How sad.*

But what happened? While he was thinking about these things, an angel of the Lord came to him in a dream. "Joseph, son of David," the angel said, "do not be afraid to take Mary as your wife. For the child within her was conceived by the Holy Spirit. And she will have a son, and you are to name him Jesus, for he will save his people from their sins" (Matthew 1:20-21, NLT).

Joseph could have said, "I believe it all, but no thank you! This is *way* above my pay grade. And what will the guys down at the work site say? They will never believe this. I just don't want to deal with that humiliation."

We need to understand this: Joseph went through life with the reputation of being married to a promiscuous woman—which of course was the opposite of the truth and of her character. And she herself went through life being considered an immoral woman.

On one occasion the Pharisees said to Jesus, "Well, at least we weren't born of fornication!" (John 8:41) Which is another way of saying, "At least we weren't born out of wedlock like You were!"

This is the kind of reputation all three had to live with. It was like the "scarlet letter" of adultery, from the Nathaniel Hawthorne novel. Considering these things, Joseph could have said, "I think I'll take a pass on that. It's going to be way too much hassle."

But to his everlasting credit, he accepted his role without a murmur of complaint and stood by Mary like a strong oak tree for the rest of his life.

That's the manhood example he set for all time. Strong. Industrious. Faithful. Protective. Obedient to God.

The whole genealogy of Jesus Christ is a picture—or rather a series of snapshots—of incredible, mind-blowing grace. Again and again, God extends grace to "nobodies" who became somebodies in His great plan.

Why do I bring this up? Because there will never be another Joseph or Mary. Those positions are already taken. They are securely tied to your nativity sets, right? That's a one-off deal.

But please hear me on this: *There will never be another you*. Not if the world went on spinning for another million years. God has a special plan and destiny for your life, and no one else in the universe can fulfill that plan. Whatever you have gone through in your life is preparation for what is still ahead. God is preparing you for your life on this planet, and for eternity to come.

And He can use you in a powerful way as well.

The Christmas story isn't about God helping perfect people but rather saving lost people. Doing for sinners what they could never do for themselves. Every one of us can touch our world. Each of us has a unique sphere of influence. We have family, friends, neighbors. We have people we work with or go to school with or even randomly meet in the course of a given day. We can impact our world.

That has been His plan and dream for us literally from day one.

Joseph was never famous in his own time and probably wasn't known outside of Nazareth. But he played the part God gave him to the best of his ability and will be remembered for it forever.

Thanks and Praise

Lord, thank You for Joseph's quiet strength—how he accepted the role and the task You gave him and stayed obedient to You through all his days. Help me find the unique plan You have in store for me. I want Heaven's direction in my life, too, today—even in the specifics.

He Is Coming Again

For the Lord himself will appear with
the declaration of victory. . .
He will descend from the heavenly realm.
1 Thessalonians 4:16, TPT

For all the effort our secular world puts into diluting or canceling the memory and traditions of Christmas, you can still see it coming.

You've probably noticed the telltale signs in your town and in your neighborhood: lights going up on houses or a manger scene in someone's yard (though not as often as in days gone by). You see Christmas trees on top of cars, traffic backing up around the stores and malls. And, of course, the nonstop commercials on TV, promoting every item or service under the sun as a Christmas gift.

The pressure is on! Everyone on all sides pushes us to get out there and spend our money to "celebrate" this season. I don't think it's possible you could miss that Christmas is here.

As we have said in this book, however, many people did miss that first Christmas, when Jesus was born in Bethlehem. In fact, most people in the world missed it.

But it's not as if the people of Israel didn't receive signs and signals that something special was in the air. Godly men and women had the sense that the coming of the Messiah was "just around the corner." And it was!

After Jesus began His ministry and met Philip, that disciple hurried off to tell his fellow townsman Nathanael about it, saying, "We have found the very person Moses and the prophets wrote about! His name is Jesus, the son of Joseph from Nazareth" (John 1:45, NLT).

The woman at the well in Sychar, even though she was a Samaritan, was also looking for the Messiah. Before she recognized Jesus for who He was, she said, "I know the Messiah is coming. . . When he comes, he will explain everything to us" (John 4:25, NLT).

There's no doubt about it: Even after 400 years of silence, some in Israel had stayed on their tiptoes, watching and waiting for the appearance of the Messiah. Going back to the story of Anna: After seeing the baby Jesus in the temple, she "spoke about the child to all who were looking forward to the redemption of Jerusalem."[31] How many was that? We don't know. But it may have been a good number.

The Hebrew prophets had clearly foretold that a Savior was coming, that He would indeed be the Messiah, that He would be born of a virgin, be a direct descendent of David, and that He would be born in the tiny village of Bethlehem.

For the most part, however, people drove right past those road signs.

Why? Because they really weren't paying attention.

Life was difficult under Roman occupation, and most people just plodded along, trying to make a living and attempting to stay out of trouble with the authorities. The Jewish leaders and scholars, though they had their heads filled with biblical content, had become completely absorbed in the minutiae of all the extra laws, regulations, and traditions added to the Law over the generations. In fact, they were so distracted that they didn't recognize the Messiah when He was standing right in front of them.

Things were spiritually dark for Israel in those days. No one had seen an angel or heard from a prophet or witnessed a miracle in living memory. Demons were at work in the land, possessing men and women in frightening ways, and inflicting diseases.

Even so, things were ripe for the arrival of the Messiah—and the godly people in the land sensed it and watched for it.

Sadly, however, many people in Israel were spiritually asleep when God visited them that first Christmas. It's pretty much the same as we look at our own culture today. Yes, we celebrate Christmas, but it is so easy to forget about Christ.

You and I, however, can make sure we are ready when He returns to the earth, as He has promised. Jesus Christ born in the manger in Bethlehem, crucified on the cross of Calvary, risen again from the dead, is coming back again.

That may not be a popular topic of discussion, but it doesn't make it any less true. Some people don't want to talk about the rapture (when Christ comes *for* His Church) or the Second Coming (when Christ comes *with* His Church) and shrug it off as a fad or of little importance. That's just what the apostle Peter said people would do.

I want to remind you that in the last days there will come scoffers who will do every wrong they can think of and laugh at the truth. This will be their line of argument: "So Jesus promised to come back, did he? Then where is he? He'll never come! Why, as far back as anyone can remember, everything has remained exactly as it was since the first day of creation. (2 Peter 3:3-4, TLB)

Those who have been watching and waiting, however, know that He will come soon—and we don't want to miss that! He came right on schedule the first time and He will come right on schedule the second time. Going back to Galatians 4:4, we read: "But when the time had fully come, God sent his Son, born of a woman" (NIV1984).

Jesus was born in Bethlehem when the time was just right. He wasn't early and He wasn't late. And it will be the same when He comes back again: He will come when the time is just right, the time set by His Father.

Sometimes, as we watch things going from bad to worse in our cities, in our nation, and in our world, we may find ourselves wondering, *Lord, are You really paying attention to planet Earth? Do You realize how bad it has gotten? Have You seen the headlines? Have You checked out what they're teaching our kids in the schools?* The answer is yes, He is fully aware of everything that is happening (and an infinite number of things we're not aware of).

Regarding the timing of His coming, Jesus said, "But of that day and hour no one knows" (Matthew 24:36, NKJV). So if you hear some teacher on the radio or preacher on YouTube who says he knows the day of the Lord's return, go ahead and change the station, click on to another video. He doesn't know what he's talking about, because Jesus says, *"No one knows."* Period.

But if we can't know the specific date, we can discern the *season* that we're in. Jesus said in Matthew 16:2-3 (NLT), "You know the saying, 'Red sky at night means fair weather tomorrow, red sky in the morning means foul weather all day.' You know how to interpret the weather signs in the sky, but you don't know how to interpret the signs of the times!"

Early this morning, it was raining outside my house. How did I know? Well, it was like this: I walked outside and it rained on me. By the way, bald men are always first to know when it's raining. I will be walking down the street with my wife and say, "It's raining." She will say, "No, it's not." But she has so much hair she wouldn't even feel the rain for a while. I will reply, "Yes, it *is* raining. I feel the drops on my head!"

No, we can't know the day or hour of Christ's return, but we can learn to read the signs of the times. And those signs have been saying consistently and clearly that the time for our Lord's return is near.

During this Christmas season, the signs are all around us. But for most people, it's just a holiday. Most of us will quickly forget the gifts we receive. In fact, we might not remember the gifts we received last year. Christmas will come and go, whether we're ready for it or not. But when it comes to Jesus Christ returning to earth, being ready couldn't be more important. People may have missed the first Christmas, but we don't want to miss His return. He is coming for those who are watching and waiting.

So don't just be ready for Christmas this year, be ready for Christ Himself.

Thanks and Praise

Dear Lord, what would I be doing if I knew for sure You were coming today? I would make sure I was ready! Help me be like Simeon and Anna, who lived out their lives with an excited expectation of Your arrival. You are coming again to take me to a new Home with You! Praise You, Jesus, for that promise.

Be Ready

"Be on guard! Be alert!
You do not know when that time will come."
Mark 13:33, *NIV*

As Christmas approaches, most of us have a "to-do" list. It's in an app on your iPhone, a sticky note on your dashboard, or a half sheet of lined paper taped to your fridge.

We want to get the house decorated, the shopping done, and maybe a menu planned for when company arrives. Maybe there are travel arrangements to be made. And these tasks must be accomplished *before* December 24! It won't help to get ready for Christmas after Christmas is over. So here's a word to the wise, especially if you're a guy: Don't let Christmas Eve come as a revelation to you. Make sure you've thought through what you're getting for your wife or your girlfriend. You'll have a happier Christmas if you are ready.

Referring to the coming of Jesus, Scripture is saying to us: Be ready to go. Have your bags packed and your shirt sleeves rolled up. Put on your comfortable shoes. Be ready to depart at a moment's notice.

This is the question we need to ask ourselves: Am I ready?

Jesus Himself gives us this reminder:

> "Be dressed for service and keep your lamps burning, as though you were waiting for your master to return from the wedding feast. Then you will be ready to open the door and let him in the moment he arrives and knocks. . . He may come in the middle of the night or just before dawn. But whenever he comes, he will reward the servants who are ready." (Luke 12:35, 36, 38, NLT)

We may find an account like this hard for us to grasp, because it is relating to a long-ago and far-away culture, back in biblical times. Jesus is describing a classic first-century Jewish wedding. Unlike our weddings today, a first-century Hebrew wedding would last *days* rather than hours—an extended time of celebration. One fun element was the fact that you didn't know when the groom would arrive. The bridal party would all be assembled, the bridesmaids prepared, and the groomsmen ready.

But where was the groom?

Without warning, someone would make the announcement: *"The groom is coming!"*

If you were asleep or off doing this or that, you might miss the ceremony. That announcement might come in the middle of the night or early in the morning at first light. You simply had to *be* ready and *stay* ready, sleeping in your wedding clothes if necessary. The groom would suddenly appear in your midst, and the ceremony would begin.

Jesus is saying, "That's how it will be when I return. Be ready. Be alert. Don't be distracted by trivialities or overly preoccupied with other things." The New King James version says: "Let your waist be girded and your lamps burning."

What does it mean to have your waist girded? People in those days wore long flowing robes, with a belt. When they wanted to cinch up their robe for easier movement, they would tuck it into their belt. This belt would also have objects attached; for instance, they would sometimes carry an extra flask of oil for their lamp. (It would be like having extra alkaline batteries for your flashlight.) Their lamp was saucer-like, filled with oil and a floating wick. When your oil got low, you would pull out your little flask and replenish your lamp.

Jesus is saying to keep your robe cinched up and tucked in your belt, so that you can move fast when you need to. In other words, put those fresh batteries in that flashlight. Gas up your car. Have your cell phone charged to the max. Be ready to roll at a moment's notice.

That is how we are to be in anticipation of our Lord's return.

When Christ comes, you won't have time to change or tweak anything. You won't be able to say, "Well, I need to wrap a couple of things up first." No, there will be no two-minute drill. There will be no time at all. It will occur in a millisecond— "the twinkling of an eye," as the Scripture says (1 Corinthians 15:52, NIV).

So just be ready and stay ready. Stay in close fellowship with your King. Because you could be walking from the kitchen into the living room and suddenly find yourself swept up into the clouds. You could be talking with a friend, open your mouth to speak, and suddenly find yourself with the Lord in the air. That is how fast the rapture will happen, and it could take place at any moment. There is nothing left on the prophetic calendar that must happen before Jesus returns for His Church.

Christ will come right on time—*His* time. The apostle Peter tells us, "The Lord isn't really being slow about his promise, as some people think. No, he is being patient for your sake. He does not want anyone to be destroyed, but wants everyone to repent" (2 Peter 3:9, NLT).

So what are we supposed to be doing until the Lord comes back? Several things, according to Luke 12. First, we are to be watching for Him. Jesus said, "Blessed are those servants whom the master, when he comes, will find watching" (v. 37, NKJV).

This doesn't mean we're to stand around like idiots staring into the sky. To "watch" simply means to be alert and aware. For instance, when I read a news website, I'm always thinking about world news and national news in terms of the "signs of the times." So I'm not just seeing another conflict in the Middle East, or reading about an economic meltdown in Europe, or noting that North Korea or Iran has threatened to use its nuclear weapons, or that evil teaching has infected our public schools. Yes, I am seeing those things. But I'm also looking for indicators—biblical signs—that the day of the Lord's return is near.

Jesus says, "So when all these things begin to happen, stand and look up, for your salvation is near!" (Luke 21:28, NLT). The Bible also says, "He will come again, not to deal with our sins, but to bring salvation to all who are eagerly waiting for him" (Hebrews 9:28, NLT).

So be watching.

If you really believe that Christ could return at any moment, this will have a practical impact on the way you live. In other words, the stronger I hold to the truth about Christ's any-moment return, the more it shapes how I live my life.

Have you ever noticed how people behave differently when a uniformed police officer enters the room? I have a few friends who are cops, and I was meeting with one for coffee the other day. So we walked into that little coffee place together, and the whole atmosphere of the room changed. People began confessing stuff to him: "I really wasn't speeding that much on my way over here . . ." He just laughed.

In the same way, knowing that Jesus could merge into our world at literally any second ought to affect the way we live, what we do, and what we say.

Scripture also tells us to *anxiously* await His return. In a sense, we should be "on pins and needles." Jesus said: "Be ready to open the door and let him in the moment he arrives and knocks" (Luke 12:36, TLB).

Have you ever looked forward to someone's arrival, and before they could even knock you opened the door? That is how we should be when we think of the return of Jesus: Looking forward to that moment with anticipation and joy, and not dreading it at all.

In the book of Revelation, in the very last two verses of the Bible, Jesus says, "Surely I am coming quickly." And the response of every true Christian will be, "Amen. Even so, come, Lord Jesus!" (Revelation 22:20, NKJV).

Anything that would prevent us from answering in that way is out of place in our lives. Anything that would make it difficult for us to say, "Come quickly, Lord Jesus" is spiritual weakness and a danger area to us.

What should we be doing as we await His return? We should be using the days and years of our lives to serve the Lord, and to look for every opportunity to tell people about Jesus.

By the way, this is a happy way to live. Luke 12:37 (NKJV) says, "Blessed are those servants whom the master, when he comes, will find watching." This verse could be translated, "*Oh how happy* are those servants."

Watching daily for the Lord's return isn't a miserable, repressive, confining way to live; it is a happy, joyful, purposeful way to live.

When you hear the Christmas carols that remind you of His first coming, as an infant in Bethlehem, let them also remind you that His next coming is just around the corner. Perhaps before you turn the calendar page to a New Year.

Thanks and Praise

Lord, I want to be ready to say a word for You today if the opportunity comes. I want to point people toward You if the door opens—whether it's a neighbor or person at work or a clerk at the store. Help me to watch for those openings, and put the right words in my mouth, I pray in Your name.

God with Us

"I will never leave you, never!
And I will not loosen my grip
on your life!"
Hebrews 13:5, TPT

Children's toys today have become unbelievably more complex and elaborate than the toys of previous generations.

Back in 1960, I remember asking—begging—for a toy called "Mr. Machine" for Christmas. (Google it. It was very low-tech but pretty cool in the day.) And I was wildly excited to discover it waiting for me that year under the tree.

As I remember, it didn't plug in and didn't have any batteries. By winding a large metal key on Mr. Machine's back, however, he would roll forward, legs and arms moving, bell ringing, and opening his mouth and "squawking." You could rotate a little wheel behind the toy to make it run in a circle or curve instead of moving in a straight line.

And that was about it.

I remember thinking that it looked so cool and futuristic, and I felt pretty happy about it until my buddy came over with *his* new toy. I had never seen anything like it: a battery-operated, plastic scuba diver, outfitted with dual tanks just like Lloyd Bridges on the old *Sea Hunt* TV series. When you turned it on, the legs kicked. You could put it in your bathtub or wading pool, and it sank to the bottom with bubbles coming out the top.

It was absolutely the edgiest technology I had ever seen. And suddenly I wasn't so happy with my Mr. Machine. I wanted a plastic scuba diver too.

The funny thing is that as you get older, things really don't change much. What's that old saying? "The only difference between men and boys is the price of their toys." And that's why Christmas is such a letdown for so many people—children and otherwise—because there is such a buildup surrounding the giving and getting of presents.

Here's the basic problem: No matter what you receive, no matter how high the price tag or elaborate the technology, "things" will always disappoint you. If that's what Christmas is all about to you, the holiday will always be a synonym for disappointment.

That's why all the people out there who work so tirelessly to take Jesus Christ out of Christmas will receive exactly what they want: a meaningless holiday with an emphasis on material possessions and acquiring stuff.

If, however, you want to have the merriest Christmas of all and experience Christmas the way it was meant to be experienced, you need to understand and embrace the essential message of the season.

Which is simply this: *Immanuel.* God is with us.

The first chapter of the Gospel of Matthew lays it out for us.

> *So all this was done that it might be fulfilled which was spoken by the Lord through the prophet, saying: "Behold, the virgin shall be with child, and bear a Son, and they shall call His name Immanuel," which is translated, "God with us."* (Matthew 1:22-23, NKJV)

Did Joseph and Mary really have any concept at all about the child who was to enter their lives? When Mary gave birth in that inhospitable place, wrapped her baby in strips of rags and placed Him in a manger, possibly in the back of some cave near Bethlehem, did she grasp who He was? Did she know that the child she nursed and held in her arms was the Savior of the world? Did she have any comprehension that her little one was *God* in human form?

Did she understand that this was Immanuel—God with us?

"God with us" is the very essence of the Christian experience. All other religions basically lay out things that you must *do* to somehow reach God or make it to Heaven or achieve Nirvana, or simply to escape wrath. You must do this and this and this and this. And if you do it all perfectly, maybe you will gain the approval of God or reach the outskirts of Heaven.

In contrast to other world religions, Christianity doesn't say "do," it says "done!" Our salvation was accomplished by God Himself, for us.

How? Immanuel, God with us, became a man and took our penalty on Himself.

Christmas is a lonely time of year for many. Some people dread the month of December, wishing they could skip right from Thanksgiving to New Year's Day. Maybe there are parents with an empty nest who miss the hustle and bustle of Christmases past. Maybe someone has lost a spouse to death and memories of Christmas only seem to make the pain and desolation harder to bear. Or perhaps a marriage broke up or has been strained, and all the holiday celebrations seem empty and sad.

Helen Glashow, an expert on bereavement, captured those thoughts when she wrote: "Christmas is a time for holidays. A time to be home. A time for families that are intact and doing cheerful and happy and fun things. But for some people it is not a time of cheer. It is a time of great pain, loneliness, separation, and anxiety."

Is that a description of you? Is this a time of anxiety or separation for you? Are you lonely and feel as though you have no one at all?

Loneliness is a painful sense of being unwanted, unloved, unneeded, uncared for, and maybe even unnecessary. Studies have shown that one of the main reasons people commit suicide is because deep down inside they are lonely.

That's why the name Immanuel is so powerful. GOD . . . IS . . . WITH . . . YOU.

Right now. Present tense. In literal reality.

He didn't just say that, He *named* Himself that. You are not alone, and that's what God would have you understand right now.

The sense of loss and the ache of loneliness may go bone-deep, but as Corrie ten Boom wrote, "There is no pit so deep God's love is not deeper still."

Jesus knows all about loneliness. He can be with you in a special way if you are feeling lonely this Christmas. Here is what Jesus has promised to every man or woman, boy or girl who has ever put their faith in Him:

> *"I will never leave you nor forsake you. . . And be sure of this: I am with you always, even to the end of the age."* (Hebrews 13:5, NKJV; Matthew 28:20, NLT)

That is the bottom line of this book and the bottom line of life itself: Jesus and Jesus alone will meet your needs. Not Christmas presents. Not Christmas movies. Not neighborhood light shows. Not even family and friends. People, even good people who love you, will let you down in some way, shape, or form. Pastors and spiritual leaders will let you down. You and I have let down people, and we've been let down by people in turn.

But Jesus will never let you down. He alone is the answer to loneliness, and He will live with you, beside you, and within you.

Thanks and Praise

Lord, if I could just see You for a moment walking beside me—if I could catch a glimpse of You sitting across this room right now, I know that nothing would make me anxious or afraid. Give me eyes of faith, Lord Jesus, to see You sharing this day with me, to feel Your hand on my shoulder, and to see Your smile.

A Friend for All Seasons

"When you're in over your head,
I'll be there with you.
When you're in rough waters,
You will not go down."
Isaiah 43:2, MSG

Did it cross your mind that Jesus of Nazareth might have been the loneliest man who ever lived?

You say, "But didn't He have disciples?"

Yes, He did.

But the Bible tells us that "Even in his own land and among his own people, the Jews, he was not accepted. Only a few would welcome and receive him" (John 1:12, TLB). The Old Testament prophet, writing of Jesus' life, said of Him: "We despised him and rejected him—a man of sorrows, acquainted with bitterest grief. We turned our backs on him and looked the other way when he went by. He was despised, and we didn't care" (Isaiah 53:3, TLB).

Those disciples of Jesus couldn't even stay awake to watch with Him in the greatest crisis of His life. And when a murderous mob descended on the Lord, they all took off to save their own skins, leaving Him to be condemned and abused, and to die.

On the cross, with His life slipping away inch by terrible inch, and bearing the weight of all the sins of all time on His shoulders, Jesus even experienced a separation from God the Father, who turned away from Him. He called out from the cross, "My God, My God, why have You forsaken Me?" (Psalm 22:1, NKJV).

Looking down the long centuries, the prophet Isaiah saw the Messiah's loneliness and grief and wrote: "He was despised and rejected—a man of sorrows, acquainted with deepest grief" (Isaiah 53:3, NLT).

Does He understand your feelings of loneliness or emptiness? Of course He does! And He wants to come alongside you today in a way that no one else in the universe can. He will be *with* you and *in* you.

Without question, that is one of the most remarkable teachings in all the Bible: that somehow, Christ Himself enters into the human heart and *lives* there.

The Bible clearly teaches this, whether we're able to wrap our minds around it or not. In fact, our Lord said in John 14:23 (NLT), "All who love me will do what I say. My Father will love them, and we will come and make our home with each of them."

Don't skim past that last sentence.

Don't let this sound like a bunch of religious jargon to you or nice words for a devotional book. It's as real as the chair you're sitting on right now, as real as the air you are drawing into your lungs. Jesus is saying, "My Father and I want to come and set up house with you. We want to live inside of you."

No, I don't understand it very well either. But I know this: No matter what, I am not alone in life and I will *never* be alone in life. And neither are you . . . no matter what you are going through right now, no matter what difficulty or crisis or heartbreak you might be facing, no matter what impossibility looms on the path ahead of you.

God is with you. Not in an abstract, theoretical way, but in fact, in truth, and in person. Remember these words from the book of Isaiah?

"When you pass through the waters,
I will be with you;

and when you pass through the rivers,
they will not sweep over you.
When you walk through the fire,
you will not be burned;
the flames will not set you ablaze."
(Isaiah 43:2, NIV)

Are you going through a river of difficulty this Christmas? Maybe you find yourself in a fire of oppression. Remember, you are not alone. God is with you.

Maybe your marriage has been badly bruised—or has fallen completely apart this year. Perhaps your children have forgotten about you. But God is with you, and He has *not* forgotten about you. Maybe you are single and wonder if you will ever find that right person you're searching for. Remember, God is with you. Maybe you are isolated in a hospital or conva-lescent home or prison cell. People write to me from these places all the time. *But you are not alone in that place.* God is—literally—with you as well. That is the essential message of Christmas: God is with us.

Have you asked Jesus into your life?

I think Revelation 3:20 is one of my favorite verses in all the Bible. In that verse, Jesus says, "Behold, I stand at the door and knock. If anyone hears My voice and opens the door, I will come in to him and dine with him, and he with Me" (NKJV).

The problem with this translation is that it sounds too formal. Who says "behold" anymore? The UPS guy with a package doesn't say "Behold" into your Ring doorbell camera.

I'm not making fun of the statement of Jesus; I'm just saying the translation doesn't relate very well. So, to bring it into modern vernacular, Jesus is saying, "I'm at the door. Open up. Hey, it's your Friend out here."

Yes, that's a loose paraphrase. But you get the idea. What is Jesus saying? He's saying, "I want to come into your life. I want to be part of everything that you're doing. Let's have a meal together. I want to spend time with you."

Personally, I don't enjoy eating with people I don't know. I keep thinking, *Maybe they're trying to sell me something.* And I just can't relax. When it comes to eating a meal, I only want to eat with someone who is a friend or family member or someone I'm comfortable with. I want to eat my food and steal some of theirs too. That's how you know you are really a good friend—when you can take the food off their plate without asking.

Jesus is saying, "Come on. Let's drop the pretenses. Let's get real here. I want to be your friend. I want to have fellowship with you. I want to spend time with you." He's saying, "I want to hang out with you. We'll order desert and some coffee. I've got all the time in the world, and I'm interested in everything you have to say. I want fellowship, friendship, and intimacy with you."

That's intimacy. That is "God With Us."

The very thought of this should touch us deeply. Just to think that God—the Almighty Creator of the universe—would be vitally interested in someone like you or me! To think that He actually wants to be part of all we say and do. How could it be true? And yet, it is true. One of the songs I like to sing at this time of year is the old Christmas hymn, "O Come, O Come, Immanuel":

> O come, O come, Immanuel,
> And ransom captive Israel
> That mourns in lonely exile here
> Until the Son of God appear.
> Rejoice! Rejoice! Immanuel
> Shall come to you, O Israel.
>
> O come, O Wisdom from on high,
> Who ordered all things mightily;

To us the path of knowledge show
And teach us in its ways to go.
Rejoice! Rejoice! Immanuel
Shall come to you, O Israel.

We sing that. But do we want that? Do we? *Do we want Immanuel to come? Do we really want Him to be part of our lives—not just at Christmas but all year long?* Christmas is coming, and like this book, Christmas is almost over. The presents will be opened, and all that pretty paper will be stuffed into the trash can at the curb, along with the tree. You'll soon be tired of those new toys and gadgets, and you'll move on to other things.

But if you have Immanuel, what does it matter?

Christmas comes and goes, but Immanuel stays. Forever.

Thanks and Praise

Lord, Your presence with me is the secret of my strength. When I feel depleted, when my spirit feels empty, when my batteries are in the red zone, You connect me with Your unlimited strength, wisdom, perspective, and joy. I rest in You today. I praise You that You are Emmanuel . . . God with me!

ONE FINAL WORD

Before you close this book, let me ask you a simple question: *Has Jesus Christ taken residence in your heart and life?*

You might say, "Well, I think He may have." Listen, if the Creator of the universe has entered your life, you will know. Here's the good news: He's just a prayer away.

Coming back to Revelation 3:20, Jesus says, "Behold, I stand at the door and knock. If anyone hears My voice and opens the door, I will come in to him and dine with him, and he with Me" (NKJV).

How do you become a Christian? How does Christ come to live in your heart? He comes when you ask Him in!

Would you like Jesus to come into your life? Would you like to have your sin forgiven? Would you like to know with certainty that you will go to Heaven when you die? Would you like to be ready for the Lord's return?

If so, pray this simple prayer with me:

Lord Jesus,
I know that I am a sinner.
But I also know that You are the Savior who died on
that cross for my sin.
I am sorry for my sin and I repent of it right now.
Come into my life, Jesus, right now.
Thank You for hearing and answering this prayer.
In Jesus' name I pray, Amen.

Did you just pray that prayer? If so, congratulations and welcome to the family of God. I would like to send you a special edition of the Bible that includes my notes. It's called *The New Believer's Bible*, and I will send you a copy at no charge.

Just contact me at Greg@Harvest.org.

And have the most joyous Christmas ever!

ABOUT THE AUTHOR

Greg Laurie is the senior pastor of Harvest Christian Fellowship with campuses in California and Hawaii. Laurie's weekly television program, Harvest + Greg Laurie, is carried on major TV networks such as Lifetime, Fox Business, Newsmax, and Daystar. Laurie has authored over 70 books including *Jesus Revolution* and *Steve McQueen: The Salvation of an American Icon*. Greg has been married to Cathe Laurie for 50 years and their life story is told in the film, *Jesus Revolution*. They have two sons and five grandchildren.

Larry Libby is an editor and collaborator who has helped Christian communicators develop and refine their messages for almost 50 years. He is also the author of several books, including *Seeing God in America* and *Someday Heaven*. He and his wife, Carol, live in Washington.

ENDNOTES

1. "Why was B.C. and A.D. changed to B.C.E. and C.E." by Izey Victoria Odiase, March 13, 2018, izeyodiase.com.

2. THE LIVING BIBLE

3. THE MESSAGE

4. 1 Chronicles 4:9-10

5. Matthew 19:26, NKJV

6. Lewis, C. S. 2012. Mere Christianity. C. S. Lewis Signature Classic. London, England: William Collins.

7. Ephesians 3:16-18, NIV

8. Lord Tennyson, Alfred 1867 "The Higher Pantheism"

9. Jonah 2:8, NIV1984 edition

10. Psalm 16:11, TLB

11. Proverbs 15:13, NIV; Proverbs 17:22, NLT

12. Luke 2:11, NKJV

13. The MESSAGE

14. Philippians 2:15, MSG

15. James 1:4, NKJV

16. Ruth 3:18, NIV
17. 1 Samuel 10:8, NIV
18. Psalm 37:7, NKJV
19. Haggai 2:7
20. Luke 2:33, MSG
21. Luke 2:34-35, NLT, emphasis mine
22. THE PASSION TRANSLATION
23. Luke 2:14, NKJV
24. Luke 2:14, NLT, emphasis mine
25. THE MESSAGE
26. Luke 2:34-35, NLT
27. Acts 16:22-34
28. Acts 16:25, NLT
29. Psalm 139:17, TLB
30. See Mark 6:3
31. Luke 2:38, NIV

Established in 1973, Harvest Ministries with Greg Laurie has made its mission to know God and make Him known. Over 50 years of church services, large-scale evangelistic events, and a multimedia platform for sharing the gospel has propelled that mission forward to all corners of the globe.

Learn more at harvest.org